OCT 2 2 2008

CONCORD

D0573466

HOW
TO HAVE
STYLE

· · · · · ·

HOW TO HAVE STYLE

isaac mizrahi

GOTHAM BOOKS

Published by Penguin Group (USA) Inc.

375 Hudson Street, New York, New York 10014, USA

Penguin Group (Canada), 90 Eglinton Avenue East, Suite 700, Toronto, Ontario M4P 2Y3, Canada (a division of Pearson Penguin Canada Inc. Penguin Books Ltd, 80 Strand, London WC2R 0RL, England; Penguin Ireland, 25 St Stephen's Green, Dublin 2, Ireland (a division of Penguin Books Ltd); Penguin Group (Australia), 250 Camberwell Road, Camberwell, Victoria 3124, Australia (a division of Pearson Australia Group Pty Ltd); Penguin Books India Pvt Ltd, 11 Community Centre, Panchsheel Park, New Delhi 110 017, India; Penguin Group (NZ), 67 Apollo Drive, Rosedale, North Shore 0632, New Zealand (a division of Pearson New Zealand Ltd.; Penguin Books (South Africa) (Pty) Ltd, 24 Sturdee Avenue, Rosebank, Johannesburg 2196, South Africa. Penguin Books Ltd, Registered Offices: 80 Strand, London WC2R 0RL, England

Published by Gotham Books,
a division of Penguin Group (USA) Inc.
First printing, October 2008

10 9 8 7 6 5 4 3 2 1

Copyright © 2008 by IM Ready Made
Gotham Books and the skyscraper logo are trademarks of
Penguin Group (USA) Inc.

Library of Congress Cataloging-in-Publication Data

Mizrahi, Isaac.
How to have style / Isaac Mizrahi.
p. cm.
Includes index.
ISBN-13: 978-1-59240-392-9 (alk. paper)
1. Clothing and dress. 2. Fashion. I. Title.
TT507.M624 2008
746.9'2—dc22
2008008991
ISBN 978-1-592-40392-9
Printed in China

The clothes and accessories seen in this book were available as of June 1, 2008. Since fashions and styles change frequently, many items may not be found in retail outlets.

While the author has made every effort to provide accurate telephone numbers and website addresses at the time of publication, neither the publisher nor the author assumes any responsibility for errors or for changes that occur after publication. Further, the publisher does not have any control over and does not assume any responsibility for author or third-party websites or their content.

Project management by Harriet Bell,
www.bellbookandhandle.com

Photography by Jason Frank Rothenberg
Inspiration board photography by Jon Shireman
Still life photography by Adrian Gaut
Photo retouching by Fanny Mavridis
How-to illustrations by Kate Francis
All other illustrations by Isaac Mizrahi

Design and production by Peter Buchanan-Smith and Josef Reyes for Buchanan-Smith LLC

contents

• • •• • •••••••••

Preface 9

Introduction **QUESTION:** HOW TO HAVE STYLE? **ANSWER:** INSPIRATION *10*

Become Inspired 14

HOW TO HAVE STYLE . . .

HOW TO HAVE STYLE . . .

I have to say something, girls.

Before you can think about having style, you have to learn to look in the mirror and like what you see. Too many women are taught to hate the way they look and are encouraged to change everything about themselves from their lips to their bust sizes. This is not that kind of book.

I can give you all my style tips and ideas about your hair, makeup, and dress, but none of this is going to do anything for you if you don't learn to accept yourself and love who you are.

I will tell you that I work with plenty of different types of women: Some skinny, some average, and some actually fat. Many times the traditional size 8 woman is the least stylish and the most self-loathing, and the woman who is more voluptuous may be radiant, stylish, and sexy because she is confident and doesn't hate what she sees every time she looks in the mirror. Children need to be told how beautiful they are again and again, until they finally believe it.

That's what *How to Have Style* is about: reinforcing everything about you that is already beautiful and reminding yourself so many times that eventually you believe that you're beautiful without me or anyone else telling you so. It sounds too easy, but accentuating what's right about you is probably harder than remedying what's wrong. Try it and keep doing it.

This is the best style advice I can give anyone.

Question:

HOW TO HAVE STYLE?

●

Answer:

INSPIRATION

. . . .
. . . .

To me, you can't have style without being inspired. When I design a new collection, I am inspired by so many things. The color of a flower. The shape of a butterfly's wing. The juxtaposition of an old tenement building next to a shiny new skyscraper. Disparate images that somehow come together and show me how to think. It's as if the ideas enter my brain and come out of my eyes and hands as sketches and ideas. I think of new ideas by reflecting on familiar thoughts and images, much the same way a chef concocts new dishes with his favorite ingredients. Somehow over the years I've become very attuned to the things that inspire me to design, to live my life, and to have style. This is what I want to share with you—the technique of identifying the things you love and learning how to let them inspire you and everything you wear.

But there's no way to unearth your personal style without first knowing who you are. Start by forgetting the idea that you look bad. You don't. I truly believe that all women are more attractive and better put together than they think they are. I don't believe in makeovers, so the women chosen to work with in the book were all good looking to begin with. I think smart women can be set free with a little friendly advice and a shot in the arm of good old-fashioned confidence. If anyone ever tries to tell you you're not pretty or that you have no sense of style, don't believe that person for a minute.

If you can accept the fact that you look just fine, it will

allow you to take the pressure off yourself and have fewer expectations. The minute that you do that, you'll be able to relax and enjoy the process of learning about style.

I'm not going to try to convince you to change yourself. I'm not one of those intolerant people who thinks that unless everyone wears my designs, or unless everyone spends most of their day getting dressed, they look awful. I like it when people look plain or messy. I applaud busy people who don't have time to think about style, as well as people who go overboard. I admire those who take risks and fail. That's the true meaning of the word "style." If you're one of those people, this book is for you.

Maybe you stopped trying at some point in your life.

Perhaps you are afraid to try something new. Or you think you don't have the time or money. Well, I know you *do* have a sense of style; you just need some help figuring out what it is, and once you figure it out, then money isn't really an issue. *How to Have Style* will encourage you to find your inspiration.

Inspiration comes from the most surprising places. When you wake up in the morning, your first impulses should not be discarded. You think "flowers." You think "stilettos." You think "gray-blue." These first thoughts need to be encouraged into physical evidence of who you are. This is your subconscious screaming out for attention. *This* is inspiration, and it needs to be respected. Inspiration is something that starts a thought process.

It motivates you to action. And it can come from any-where. It may come from the image of your favorite style icon in a magazine one day, or from a particular shade of blue in a Matisse painting the next. Or perhaps your style is motivated by a pair of red patent sandals in a store window you pass on your way to work. Wherever your inspiration comes from, you have to acknowledge that you've started a personal style puzzle. The fun part is putting all the pieces together.

Let me give you an example. The other evening, be-fore going out, I tried on every single jacket I own until I found the perfect companion to the ankle-length pants and silver moccasins I wanted to wear that evening. It was the shoes that *inspired* me to have fun with my look, and I was determined to solve this puzzle and put the whole look to-gether. By the time you've finished reading this book, you'll be inspired to look at your own style in a fresh new way.

I reached out to twelve women whose style challenges seem to resonate with everyone. The questions these twelve women asked me are universal; they're the style questions I'm asked over and over. How can I . . .

… dress stylishly on a budget?

… find clothes for my petite figure?

… pack for business trips and stay stylish?

… be stylish after 50?

… be a stylish mom?

… look great if I wear a size 12 or larger?

… introduce colors into my wardrobe?

… shop like a stylist?

… dress to express my personality?

… dress for evening?

… find my own sense of style?

… awake from my jeans coma?

Any of these questions sound familiar?

The women who appear in this book are real. None of them are stylists. None of them have more than an av-erage amount of time to devote to putting themselves to-gether. None of them had unrealistic expectations about the results.

To help them find their own style, I gave each woman a corkboard and asked her to transform it into her own personal inspiration board, about which you'll read more later. Each inspiration board is as unique, fascinating, and individual as each woman herself. The boards reveal how each woman sees herself, how she wishes to appear to others, and what she aspires to when it comes to hav-ing style.

In working with these twelve women, along with a staff including a fashion stylist, hairstylists, and a make-up artist, it became clear that certain topics needed clari-fication. In looking at other style books and at TV shows, I was baffled by all the confusing and often conflicting information. I challenged myself and my staff to address these baffling style topics throughout the book.

Between the stories of the twelve transformed women and information on important topics, you'll find that this book covers all the style essentials. One thing all of these twelve women and every other stylish woman have in common is the need to put herself first on her list of style priorities. Not the clothes or the makeup or the acces-sories, but herself. Which means you.

By reading this book, you and I are starting a dia-log about style. Even after you've finished reading, let's keep it going. Visit my websites (watchisaac.com and howtohavestyle.com) and let me know how you're doing. Because each day brings new inspirations, and new ways to use them.

BECOME

the inspiration
board

To help you discover your style, you need to know what inspires you—what colors you love, what images you are drawn to, which movies you watch over and over and love more each time. Well, you get the idea. So, buy a large corkboard and some pushpins. For a week or a month, or however long it takes, collect visual images that *inspired*

Some suggestions for finding visual inspiration and images:

- A room you'd like to live in
- Advertisements
- Architecture
- Arts and crafts stores: yarn, beads, ribbons, etc.
- Book jackets
- Cartoons
- Catalogs and junk mail
- CD/album covers
- Design and style blogs
- Fabric swatches
- Family albums
- Fashion and celebrity icons
- Flowers
- Furniture
- Google images
- Maps
- Movies
- Museums
- Nature: seashells, leaves, fruits, vegetables, etc.
- Paint-color swatches
- Paintings and sculpture
- Paper ephemera, invitations, brochures, wrapping paper
- Photographs
- Postcards of places you've been or would like to go
- Pottery and china
- Scarves
- Stationery
- Typefaces
- YouTube

speak to you and place them randomly on your board. Perhaps you already have some inspirational visuals hanging above your desk, stuck on your fridge, or decorating your bedroom mirror. Your board will change as your moods do. It will be a constant reflection of your thoughts and feelings. It will be an organized collection of all the things you see that inspire you. My inspiration board hangs in my kitchen and changes as I acquire new images or swatches.

Where to look for inspiration? Maybe you find the subtle hues of roses inspiring, or the clean silhouettes of midcentury furniture. Your possibilities are truly endless. Artists often organize their thoughts by placing bits and pieces on an inspiration board to inform their work. Think of yourself as this constantly changing canvas, one with moods and contexts. One great way to keep everything together is by faithfully keeping these inspirations on a board.

The idea is not to think just about fashion, but to collect ideas from everywhere and everything that inspires you.

Creating an inspiration board, answering the questionnaire, and reading this book will encourage you to think in visual and stylish ways.

Is red a prominent color on your inspiration board? When you open your closets and drawers, are there any maroon, cardinal, pomegranate, crimson, candy apple, fire engine, or cherry reds to be found? No? Be inspired to try on sweaters, shirts, and dresses in those shades the next time you go shopping. Did you pin advertisements of three-inch heels to your board but your shoe rack holds only flats? Guess what? It's time to move that wishful thinking from your board to your feet. Buy a pair of killer heels and start practicing how to walk in them. Is your board predominantly about flowers and birds? Perhaps that suggests that you should dress more casually or look for bright bird and colorful flower prints. It can be that simple. You'll be surprised how your eyes will be opened up to who you are once you complete your inspiration board.

the photograph

S omewhere—perhaps hidden away with old letters or in a family album—is a favorite photograph of yourself. You know the one. You look at it and think, "Wow, I looked good then." This special photograph may not be about how old you were, or what you were wearing, but rather how you felt at that particular moment and how the camera captured your personality. It's that personality and those feelings we want to recapture. Find that picture and keep it with you to remind yourself how gorgeous you *really* are.

· · · · · · · · · · · · · · ·

the questionnaire

T he next step is for you to fill out my style questionnaire. If you pay attention to the right questions and the answers, they could change your life. If nothing else it will make you aware of your habits. When you answered the question "Who is your style inspiration?" perhaps it was with someone you know or a famous style icon. Think about how you can translate that vision to yourself and make it come true. Each chapter begins with a question from the questionnaire that seemed most relevant to the story about the change the woman underwent.

Certain questions, certain answers that you come up with will resonate more than others. That is the information I want you to notice first. The issues that made you think the most are the issues you need to deal with the most.

If you answered that your legs are your best feature, for example, do everything style smart to accentuate them. Wear short skirts, high heels, and opaque tights instead of pants and flats. If you haven't had a bra fitting in five years, get one at a department store.

This is not a magazine survey where you add up points at the end to find out if you're stylish or not. This is a tool to help you start thinking. Thinking about style issues. Thinking about your tastes. Thinking about yourself.

Once your questionnaire is complete, put the answers aside for a day or two. By giving yourself breathing room, you'll be able to revisit the questionnaire with a fresh eye. Then you'll be on your way to understanding your answers to the style questions and identifying the contexts of looks, and the looks that fit those contexts.

· · · · · · · · · · · · · · ·

the questionnaire

· · · · · · · · · · · · · ·

Answer the questions in the questionnaire below. Write down whatever comes
into your head. Some of the questions (and your answers) may seem irrelevant, but trust me,
your answers will help you discover your personal style.

DESCRIBING YOUR STYLE

1	What colors do you wear most frequently?
2	Which color combination(s) do you wear most frequently?
3	From your teeth to your toes, lips to legs, what's your favorite body part?
4	What's your least favorite? And the part you try to camouflage?
5	What would you never be caught wearing?
6	What would you never leave the house without putting on?
7	What are five clothing/fashion items you can't live without?
8	What's the one item in your closet that you wear again and again and again?
9	What do you splurge on? Handbags? Jeans? Shoes? Makeup? Other?
10	What would you never spend a lot of money on? Handbags? Jeans? Shoes? Makeup? Other?
11	What's your biggest style challenge?

| 12 | How much time do you spend getting ready for work? For a night out? |

| 13 | When was the last time you were professionally measured and fitted for a bra? |

| 14 | What was the last clothing/accessory purchase you made? |

DISCOVERING YOUR STYLE

| 15 | If you had to choose one favorite color, what would it be? |

| 16 | When you get dressed, who are you dressing for? Yourself? The community you live in? |

| 17 | Why does your favorite painting or photograph appeal to you? |

| 18 | Who is your style inspiration? |

| 19 | When you were a little girl, who did you dream of looking like? Did you try to copy the style of anyone in particular? |

| 20 | What is the first thing you think of in the morning? |

| 21 | What look or style have you always wanted to try but have never had the nerve? |

| 22 | How do you think people see you style-wise? |

| 23 | What's the one thing you'd like to tell the world? |

| 24 | How do you want to be remembered style-wise? |

feeling it

One of the first things to make clear when discovering your sense of style is figuring out who and what to believe. You have to relearn how to look at yourself in the mirror. Ask yourself, "What do I like? What kinds of clothes, accessories, and colors appeal to me?" You have to keep answering those questions. It doesn't matter what you think others will like, or what you think you're expected to like. What do *you* really like? What do *you* love? The big, big question is, if you're not sure, how do you figure out what's right? Do you believe the saleswoman in a store trying to sell you clothes or makeup? Think about it. Isn't her real motive to sell you merchandise, no matter how objective she claims to be? Can you trust your mother or your husband, who, let's face it, has a particular way she or he wants you to look that complies with their idea of who you are? While they may have good intentions, it's hard for your nearest and dearest to step back and give you a truly objective opinion.

So how do you know when something is right?

The only way to really know is to feel it in your gut.

When looking for a new apartment or a house, you spend a lot of time going to open houses, walking in and out of dozens of places. When you find the right place, you know in your gut it's right and you think, "I can happily live here."

It's the same with clothes, accessories, hair, and makeup. I want you to train yourself to react emotionally when you look at a pair of shoes or a shade of blonde. Learn to listen to that inner voice that tells you when a jacket, a handbag, or a lipstick color is right or wrong.

The more you do this, the easier it will become. When you stand in front of a mirror deciding which shoes to wear or if the hose you selected look right for the occasion, the answer will come from your instincts, which you are beginning to identify, discover, and hone. As you learn to trust yourself, the process will become so second nature you won't even have to think about it. Suddenly, you will know how to have style.

You have to try on clothes. Lots of clothes. I'm so sick of hearing, "I hate trying on clothes." That has to change. Make it fun. Go to lunch with a friend and spend the afternoon going from store to store and trying on clothes. If you're not willing to make an investment of time, then close this book. I can't help you.

• Remember that intimidating boutique you always drive or walk by and think, "Cool stuff in the windows." Go in. Don't buy anything on the first visit. Start with a conversation. Ask for the owner or manager, and tell her you want a new look. Make it clear that you're looking for a style partnership and that if she's honest about what looks great on you, you will become a regular customer.

• I'm as wary of personal shoppers as anyone, but a personal shopper at a department store can be great. The service is complimentary, so go in and get to know one or two of them. If you develop a relationship, it can be the next best thing to having me help you decide what to wear. A talented personal shopper will listen well and interpret your style personality rather than impose hers. These relationships take time to develop, so take it one step at a time. Before you know it, you'll have your own inner sense of what's right and what's wrong.

Oh sure, you're thinking, that personal shopper just wants me to buy a lot of stuff. Yes, she's there to sell, but she benefits so much more by gaining your trust—and a regular customer. Her customers are a reflection of her and her store, so a personal shopper wants you to look good.

Sally Cunningham is a personal shopper with twenty years of experience. The way Sally sees it, "Once a good personal shopper gets to know you, she can guide you in a new direction, advise on when to make that extra investment in an instant classic, or honestly tell you when something looks truly terrible. Since I know what my clients already have in their closets, I can help to build their wardrobes from season to season."

Make an appointment ahead of time. Your personal shopper will greet you on your first visit, and together you will walk the floor, choosing from a wide array of clothes so she can gauge what appeals to you and what doesn't. (When's the last time someone did that with you?) You

find your own style team

"Personal style is what comes out when you discover your likes and dislikes, your own sense of what's right and what's wrong. This applies to clothing, cooking a meal, arranging a bouquet—anything and everything."

"Sometimes a desired look is just wrong, especially when it comes to the trendy look of the season. Know when a particular style doesn't work for you and pass on it. Confidence and knowing what's right for you is 95 percent of style."

will be whisked into a private dressing room with all the items arranged on a rack. If a dress is the wrong size, color, or fit, your personal shopper will exchange it for another. A seamstress will be summoned if alterations are necessary. If what you see and try on doesn't feel comfortable, try another store. But do be open-minded; the whole point is to try something new.

A personal shopper is there for *you*. Not the other way around. Don't be intimidated and don't let her steer the ship too much. Remember, it's your personal style, not hers. And a bonus: Once you get to know one another, your personal shopper will call or drop you a note when new merchandise arrives or a sale is coming up.

• Families are great for a telephone plan, but leave them home when shopping for a new look. Since the goal is to get out of the same old fashion rut, you don't want your mom or husband perpetuating the myth of the old you. Perhaps you have a friend whose opinion you trust. That is the person to take shopping with you and have fun with. But no matter what, rely on your own intuition and knowledge about what looks good on you.

• "Can I show you our new spring colors?" "There's an eyeliner that will make your eyes stand out. Please have a seat." Ah, yes, the siren call of the cosmetics salesperson luring you to her stool for a makeover. By the time you're all spackled and painted, your wallet is several hundred dollars lighter, and you look like a drag queen.

Most of the women in this book are wearing less makeup in their reveal photos than in their original pictures. When they first came to my studio, their eyebrows were plucked like chickens. Pearly highlighters under eyebrows, taupe and frosted ginger lipsticks, and heavy foundations made them look years older than they were.

Step away from that particular cosmetics counter. That salesperson has to reach a certain dollar goal every day, but who says you have to help her achieve her numbers? We can all tell when someone is trying to push products on us.

Before you go to the makeup counter, have a good idea of the look you want. Bring along photographs from magazines with looks that appeal to you. Discuss your

color likes and dislikes. Ask someone you can trust to ac-
company you for an honest opinion. After a few visits to
a particular store, if there's a saleswoman who earns your
trust, forge a relationship with her.

• When you see someone with a fabulous haircut, ask
her who cuts and/or colors her hair. Trust me, she'll be flat-
tered. If you're nervous about trying a new hairstylist, then
make an appointment for a ten-minute consultation. Take
some photos of hairstyles you like and discuss with the
stylist if they will work with your hair's texture and your
bone structure. Remember, it's just hair. If you don't like
the cut, the hair will grow back.

• • • • • • • • • • • • • •

W hen trying clothes, makeup, and hairstyles, it is
important that you take the stress out of the situation by putting off a final decision for as long as possible.
Why? Because eventually the decision will make itself.

If you keep looking in the mirror—looking and looking—the right choice will make itself clear. Just keep
looking until your inner eye sees what it wants to see.

I had each woman experiment with lots of different clothes and accessories, and we took photographs of
what worked and what didn't. I had them try on dozens
of shoes. Different cuts and styles of jeans went on, came
off, went on, came off. Scarves were tied and untied. One
bra was replaced with another, and another, until the perfect fit or the right peek-a-boo element was found. Handbag after handbag was paired with each outfit. Hair was
cut and styled, then cut and styled some more. Lipstick
colors were applied and wiped off, and more shades went
on, until the style lightbulb lit up.

This is when the secret-weapon phrase "just looking" was used. We were "just looking" to see what looked
and felt right.

You have to do the same thing: Try on lots of dresses,
skirts, jeans, hosiery, coats, shoes, boots, dresses, and
blouses, and keep trying them on until you say, "That's
it! Perfect!"

• • • • • • • • • • • • • •

just looking

the style team

RYAN COTTON/HAIRSTYLIST

Ryan, who works in a New York salon and styles for many photo shoots, is passionate about teaching women the importance of having a great cut and the right color.

"Every women should have a style specifically tailored to the texture of her hair, flattering to her bone structure, and age appropriate.

"Working collaboratively with Isaac and the other team members was a unique experience. Isaac really listened to what each woman wanted, yet he suggested ideas that they wouldn't have dreamed of doing

on their own. When we cut off Susan Shapiro's hair, she totally changed as a person. Not just a physical change, but a complete personality change. Be like Susan: Own your haircut."

KRISTEN NAIMAN/FASHION STYLIST

Kristen is a New York-based fashion stylist. She's a contributor to many magazines and consults for both private clients and fashion companies.

"When I look in the closet every morning, I ask myself, 'What version of myself do I want to be today? What mix feels right, makes me comfortable for the people I'll be

seeing, for the places I'll be going? Is it Lucite beads, leopard print heels, a cinched-waist dress, or a striped sailor shirt?' The answer has to be right for only that day. Asking the question and embracing the answer *is* having style.

"I love working with Isaac because he knows that the answer to this question has to come from yourself. By paying attention to the world around you, by believing that what you see is worth seeing, and by being totally open to whatever strikes your fancy, you develop what in our business is called 'your eye.' Isaac under-

stands that the skill of looking lasts your whole life, and that what you see changes as much as you do, as much as the world around you does."

MALLY RONCAL/MAKEUP ARTIST

Mally is makeup artist to the stars. She has done the makeup for many of my shows.

"I am a girl's girl to the core. I love educating and teaching women how to be their own makeup artists and make themselves the most beautiful they can be. Hey, when you look good, you feel good. You know the feeling. And when you feel

good, then you are empowered to be the best you can be.

"Isaac shares my philosophy. He has such an incredible eye and intuition. He knows how to make a woman feel stylish and beautiful and empowered by her style and beauty. And Isaac cares: It's in his soul."

YOURS TRULY

I started designing clothing when I was a tiny kid. I don't know where the process began. All I know is where it led, and I'm in the middle of it. The constant, nagging, crazy question in my life is "What is style?" I don't

know who first posed it. I don't know the definitive answer, or if I'll ever answer the question once and for all. The answer is always changing; that's the challenge of my life, chasing that answer. It's a quest, like King Arthur looking for the Holy Grail.

I help people find their style. I design clothes, accessories, home furnishings, costumes — anything, really, that needs designing, I design. And I try to have fun in the process. Sometimes it's agonizing, other times it's very rewarding. But the question "What is style?" is something that challenges me. For better or worse.

the process

All twelve women who participated in this book did exactly what I'm asking you to do: created an inspiration board, brought along a favorite picture of herself, and filled out the questionnaire.

Each woman brought her inspiration board and questionnaire to my studio, where I asked even more questions as I studied their boards. We chatted about everything regarding style and what their issues were. Then we talked about how my team and I could bring out the best in each one of them. Each one was eager to try something new—fulfilling a fantasy, discovering clothes that just weren't right—even if it was out of her usual comfort zone.

About six weeks later, we gathered in the studio, which had been transformed into a huge photography set. There was a separate staging area for Ryan to style hair and for Mally to do her makeup magic. Kristen and I handpicked clothes, shoes, and accessories for each woman. Racks, boxes, bins, and bags lined the room.

Upon arrival, each woman tried on lots of different clothes to see what worked and what didn't,

what made her feel good and what didn't. Then it was off to hair and makeup. Throughout the day, I asked again and again, "How about dyeing your hair a darker color?" "What about just wearing dresses?" "Speak up if you don't like something."

The hours passed in a frenzy of color, cutting, styling, zipping, snapping, buttoning, and buckling, along with some ooh-ing, aah-ing, and some "I don't think so's". By the time we were done, each inspiration was made real. And each

metamorphosis. Even I was amazed.

Take this process to heart. Set up your own studio at home. Make sure there's a full-length mirror and plenty of light. Set up an iron and ironing board. Take that sewing kit down from the shelf; use those pins to find the right skirt or trouser lengths for your silhouette. Invite your always-honest-with-you best friend over for the afternoon. Tell her you want the truth, nothing but the truth, about every garment you try on. By the end of the day, you too will be amazed how much

Manning's inspiration board

Waffle House • Whoopie cushion • John and Manning • Chris Rock • Black Crowes • engagement parties and weddings •
dancing on the roof • "Magnificent" nail file • "fabulous" bookmark • Cameron Diaz • Africa

Question 11

"What is your biggest style challenge?"

"I wish I had my own style that others wanted to emulate; instead, I tend to wear what's easy and inexpensive, and I always just get by. I would be thrilled to find my signature style and break out of the pack, but I have limited resources."

Manning Fairey, 27

At our first meeting, Manning told me that she works at a public relations firm, and as she climbs the corporate ladder, she wants to uncover her own core style to carry her from office to evening events and parties. She needs to do this on a just-married, just-starting-a-career budget.

Get in line—Manning and the rest of the world.

But Manning is also a free spirit. She was a ski bum for a year, backpacked through Europe, honeymooned in Africa. She always moves to her own tomboyish-Annie Hall beat. Well, almost always. When it comes to style, she's a prisoner of the ordinary: Black pants or jeans, some tops, and a few party dresses. Even with colors, it's middle-of-the-palette all the way—brown, black, and quiet earth tones. Manning didn't wear much makeup— just clear lip gloss and some mascara.

She and her husband, John, do a lot of socializing. Summers are crammed with cocktail parties and weddings; autumn is tailgating time. And then there are all those holiday get-togethers.

Too often Manning has relied on the fashion advice of others. "If someone tells me something looks good on me, then I wear it." Ready, eager, and willing, Manning kept saying, "I'll do whatever y'all say." Sorry, Manning, but that attitude wasn't doing much for you.

Please, Manning, I'm dying to know, "How do you want to look and be remembered? Who are you dressing for? Who are you trying to relate to when you put yourself together? What do you want to say about yourself? How do you see yourself? Who *are* you?"

Manning's inspiration board showed the way, with a love of sports and whimsy. She collects pottery and wears her grandmother's vintage jewelry. She has a tomboy-Southern vibe.

"I want to be fresh, original, honest, and wholesome."

Her board reiterated that message. Manning can do it. And on a budget. Tall and pretty, with a great figure, gorgeous eyebrows, and full lips, all she needed was a little drawing out. To me, there's nothing sexier than honesty and wholesomeness. Manning's inspirations brought her to new heights of style.

CUT HAIR TO CHIN

RED LIPS.

*TRY BANGS?

ACCENTUATE BUST. BRAS!

COAT IN A COLOR

SMALL HEEL? (OXFORD.)

makeup: trick of the eye

- Nothing is more chic than a well-defined brow, and Manning's was almost perfect. Just a bit of tweezing to get rid of some stray hairs, a few strokes of brow pencil, and some brow gel to hold them in place. It is important to leave some reality in eyebrows—don't go crazy and overpluck them into perfection.

- Ignore the common advice to use concealer that is two shades lighter than your foundation. That's how you end up with raccoon eyes! Use a powder concealer that matches your skin tone and is the same color as your powder foundation. Apply the concealer with a brush before any foundation.

- Manning was concerned about the bags under her eyes. Bags? What bags? Even if she had them, using the wrong concealer at her age would only emphasize them. Mally's tip for refreshing tired eyes is to soak chamomile tea bags in ice water—as cold and as icy as possible. Lie down, place the tea bags on your closed eyes, and rest for five minutes while fantasizing about the fabulous evening ahead.

BEFORE

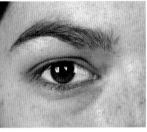

AFTER

STEP 1:
building
blocks

Especially on the weekends—when you have the most fun—start with sexy, fun, and carefree undergarments like Manning's extra-cute red bra and panties. What are you saving them for?

One of my favorite fashion tricks is to wear all one color on top (for instance, red) and another (navy) on the bottom, allowing the eye to travel up and down smoothly.

Trouser-cut, hip-skimming jeans ($129.99) flatter her hips and butt, unlike the two-sizes-too-big pants and jeans she used to wear. In this case, spending a little more on jeans makes good foundation-building sense. Navy Keds are inexpensive classics. (Manning wears a not-easy-to-find size 11 shoe. Have the same problem? Internet shopping is the answer. These were found at barefoottess.com.) The bra and hoodie peek through the Russian-red driving coat and balance a tomboy look with something girly and feminine. The whole package is wrapped up with a big scarf in different shades of red. Well-made cashmere, like this hoodie, can be found everywhere, so there's no reason to buy cheap fabrics just because you're on a budget.

"WHAT'S YOUR LEAST FAVORITE PART OF YOUR BODY? THE PART YOU TRY TO CAMOUFLAGE?"

"Breasts!"

In this outfit, the hoodie is unzipped, so the bra becomes a feature of the outfit. Manning, like many large-breasted women, wore clothes that were too big. Big clothes only make you look bigger! Manning's pants were too large, she was swimming in her shirt, and her sweater didn't come anywhere near her body. Go figure, most women want to wear a smaller size!

"Be comfortable in your own skin, that's the first rule."

STEP 2: where'd you get that?

Manning told me that she wanted to look "fresh, original, wholesome, and honest!" And stay within budget. No problem!

Her striped Marni skirt was found on eBay for $40. Just because the skirt is two seasons old doesn't mean it is passé. It's a classic.

How to shop on eBay? Easy. Go to high-end stores and try on a bazillion things by your favorite designers just to know what size you are in that brand. Perhaps your numero uno designer cuts her clothes a size larger than you usually wear. Then, on eBay, search by designer, not by category. If you search by "skirts," let's say, you'll be scrolling until 2012. As you look for your heart's desires, note which sellers carry your faves. Build a relationship with those dealers; they'll contact you when particular pieces come in, and maybe you'll even be able to bargain with them.

The blazer (page 40) is a boy's size 18; no need to shorten the sleeves, since they're already a three-quarter length. Note the pink pocket hankie—a sweet, feminine touch. Her white shirt ($59.50) is tucked in to show off her waist. The look comes together with faux tortoiseshell peep-toe flats ($29.99) and a few inexpensive, playful charm bracelets ($60).

STEP 3: boys to women

Visit the boys' sections in department and men's stores for less expensive jackets and blazers. Pick up a boy's tuxedo jacket to wear with jeans or trousers. Manning's tuxedo from the boys' department at Brooks Brothers was nearly perfect. Just the pants were cuffed. The tux with cummerbund offers a touch of man-style, yet the look is totally feminine, with high heels (below), a black lacy camisole over the same red bra, and a big red flower. The monogrammed charm bracelets do double duty; choose jewelry wisely to make it go from day to night.

Chic on the cheap

- Have a shoemaker add rubber soles and small heels to a pair of inexpensive brocade or beaded slippers.
- Try Indian stores for scarves, bangles, and accessories; Chinese shops for slippers, jade jewelry, and silk pajamas; Mexican boutiques for silver jewelry, belts, and skirts; and Moroccan boutiques for leather sandals, scarves, and big beads.
- Scour local shops for inexpensive finds: hunting and fishing stores for colorful rain boots. Army-Navy outlets for high-waisted sailor jeans. Garden shops for weekend rubber clogs.
- Buy extra-large cashmere sweaters and oxford cloth shirts in the kids' department. They'll fit just as well. They are just as well made as the adult ones . . . and half the price.
- Inexpensive tango, jazz, tap, and ballroom dance shoes come in different heel heights and looks (open or closed toe, for instance) and in an array of colors and prints that look great at the present moment.

which shoes?

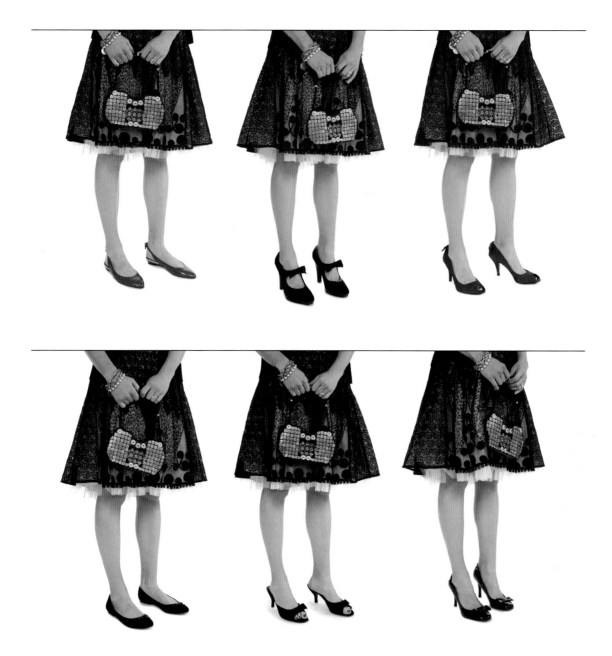

Manning looked so darn cute, no chance I'd allow her to mess up this outfit with the wrong shoes.
She tried on every pair of black and red flats, heels, sandals, slides, and slingbacks in the joint. The red slingback flats and
black mules are casual. The black platform pumps with bows are cute. All are good choices, rather than just one
right look: It all depends on where she's going. She's the only one who can feel what's the "right-est." Do the same—
stand in front of a mirror and try on every pair of shoes in your closet that might go with your outfit. You never know.
That cute evening handbag she's carrying? Just $25 at an Indian sari shop.

a little less tux

By replacing the tuxedo pants and jacket with a lacy skirt and a short-sleeved sweater, Manning gets a whole new look and a more girly version of the male-inspired tuxedo look. Everything else—red bra, black camisole, white shirt, red flower, and black cummerbund—creates another elegant evening look. A little about breasts and playing them up: For most women, if there's one bit of advice I could offer, it would be to love your breasts.

"WHAT'S YOUR FAVORITE BODY PART?"

"Lips"

"It's always better to play up your best features. In Manning's case, her lush lips filled in with a bright red lipstick and her gorgeous eyebrows are the features to emphasize. I love a red lip."

Ta-da!

COZY-SEXY

Layers of red are balanced with
denim trousers and navy sneakers.
Total cost: $303.

• • •

MORNING TO NIGHT

She can go from the office to work-related
events to dinner with this look.
Total cost: $335.

• • •

Are You Inspired?

"Isaac showed me that there is a right way and wrong way to spend money on clothes, and now I feel like I finally get that. I can look great and not always have to shop at Prada or Gucci. I feel like I'm now in control of how I dress and how I present myself to the world. I was wearing all the wrong things, and Isaac showed me the right way. I now buy clothes that are my actual size, instead of baggy pieces that looked sloppy. Now it feels weird if I don't tuck in my shirt. Since I learned to embrace higher-waisted clothes, I love the way they embrace me back."

YOUTHFUL ELEGANCE

Red bra, flower, toes, and lips add brightness to Manning's chic tuxedo paired with strappy jeweled pumps. **Total cost: $475**.

• • •

TWO FOR ONE

Get another evening look by pairing the same blouse, bra, and bag with a black-lace-over-beige-lining skirt, elbow-length cardigan, and black heels. **Total cost: $175.**

• • •

Janine's inspiration board

Halle Berry • *A Place in the Sun* • black-and white-decor • Nella Larsen • patterns and prints •
chocolate and beige • calla lily • tulips • *Laura*

Question 11

**"What's your biggest
style challenge?"**

*"Although I've
changed careers,
I don't know how to
make the transition
from a dressed-
down editor to a
professional-looking
therapist. Also, I'm
tiny and nothing
fits me."*

Janine Gardner, 30

When you are petite, people often treat you like a child. ("Oh, you're so cute and little.") Not good. Especially if you're a therapist, like Janine, who, at 4 feet 11 inches, has to look every inch the mature professional to her clients.

Clothes can do a lot of things, but they can't make you taller. They can, however, make you *seem* taller.

Making the career transition from editor to therapist was easier for Janine than making the wardrobe transition. Her too-short sweater dress (it actually is a sweater, but it's big enough to be a dress on her!) didn't give off much of a trustworthy, you-can-tell-me-everything feeling. She favored low-cut tops and too-short skirts. It certainly wasn't how I want my shrink to look.

It was time for some style therapy.

For Janine, shopping for clothes was often a disaster because of her petite frame. And, even worse, she received little sympathy from those around her, who usually said, "I wish I were a size 2."

But shopping exclusively in the children's department when you're thirty years old is a problem; no woman should have to do that.

Janine's inspiration board and questionnaire showed a love of 1940s (*Laura*) and 1950s (*A Place in the Sun*) films. Those midcentury looks—neck scarves and waist-cinching belts—can be updated for today. Her inspiration board also shows she's already good at putting colors together.

BRING NECKLINES UP OR DOWN. EMPHASIZE LONGER LINE.

EMPHASIZE LIPS.

*TAKE AWAY JANINES CURLING IRON. MAKE HAIR SPIKY.

STRAIGHTER SKIRT. SLIGHTLY LONGER.

OR FULLER SKIRT. NOT TOO LONG. SOFT COLOR. PEACH.

*TRY PANTS HEMMED TO TIP OF SHOE. (COVERING HEEL.)

makeup:
almond eyes and lush lip

Janine's classic almond eyes pop with eyeliner top and bottom, a soft beige eye shadow on her lids, and a gentle brown shadow in the crease.

There are two ways to wear lipstick as an accessory: Change your shade to go with the seasons, the time of day, or what you're wearing—Janine's lipstick goes with her red-orange scarf. Or make one particular hue your signature color and wear it all the time and with everything.

hair:
"I'd love a Halle Berry look."

Ryan first trimmed Janine's hair to give it more shape. Because her hair was chemically relaxed, dry, and brittle, he added sheen, shine, and softness with Tui hair oil. He then wrapped her hair and combed it flat to follow the shape of her head. The spiky look comes from just working the hair up and out.

STEP 1:
starting from the top

Most women wear a black skirt or pants–for a slimmer and taller look.
Switch it up and start with a black top, like this T-shirt-cut sweater with embroidered floral embellishments,
and then add colors around it. A feminine, flattering low—but not low-cut—
neckline is more professional.

STEP 2: add color

Any number of scarves work with this look— that does sometimes happen! Go for a contrasting color. A matching mint green would be too grannyish.

STEP 3: stand taller

When you're petite, finding shoes for small feet is also a struggle. Check out Giordano's at petitefeet.com.

Janine looks taller when wearing a pale, almost-naked shoe that elongates her legs. These jeweled slides are perfect. Never, ever slip on a pair of shoes like these without a fresh pedicure.

And do I have to say anything about hair removal on the entire leg? I didn't think so. It's not okay to shave only from the knee down.

JUST LOOKING

which one?

The dominant colors in this dress
are brown, cream, gray, and pink,
some of Janine's favorites. But what
color for her sweater? Try two on
at the same time. The dark brown
one dulls the whole effect, while the
light gray sweater brightens up the
dress and fits Janine better. It's all
about choosing the right shade, not
just the right color.

STEP 4: does it need something?

Alone, this dress is fine, but it needs finish, don't you think?

The yellow coat is just too much fabric for Janine's petite frame.

The sweater breaks up the stripes, allowing the introduction of the handbag pattern.

Contrary to common wisdom, wide-leg jeans are not just for tall people. Because these jeans fit properly and are hemmed to the proper length, they give Janine a long, straight line and stature.

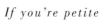

If you're petite

- To create the illusion of longer legs, draw the eye up with well-fitting clothes. Avoid clothes that are loose and flowing; they will drown you.
- Vertical, never horizontal, stripes impart a longer, leaner look.
- When it comes to petite clothing, make sure all the tailoring details—collars, pockets, cuffs, and even buttons—are proportionally scaled down.
- Wear heels.
- The right pant length is crucial; the break should cover the top of your boots or shoes.
- Wear small prints and patterns; huge ones will overwhelm you.
- Find a great tailor or seamstress (page 166).
- Check out petite fashion websites and blogs.

"To create your own style, think about yourself and take pleasure when shopping. When most people go shopping, the immediate response is to get it over with. 'Okay, I'll take it' is too often the reaction, without giving any thought as to why you're buying that particular item. Instead, stop and ask yourself, 'Where does this dress/handbag/sweater fit in my life?' If you don't have a good reason for buying it, put it back."

Hooray!

SEPARATE PIECES

Conventional wisdom says small women should wear
one color from head to toe. Wrong! Separates in
different colors don't chop her in half.

• • •

DRESSED-UP JEANS

It's all about the right proportions—right pant length,
right boot height, right jacket, and the right bag.

• • •

Are You Inspired?

"I never thought I could look great all the time, day in, day out. I just didn't think it was important. Boy, was I wrong!
Now every day is special. I feel polished, sophisticated, and confident, which is how a therapist needs to present herself to clients.
And now people don't just see me differently, they treat me differently. It's important for every woman to realize that
feeling good about yourself comes from looking good. I've never felt more inspired in my life!"

THE RIGHT STRIPES

Vertical, never horizontal, stripes when you're petite.
Let your handbag make a big statement.

• • •

SKIRT THE ISSUE

Skirts that hit just above or below the knees work for Janine.
She has to stay away from anything longer or shorter.

• • •

Bianca's inspiration board

Habitat for Humanity • The ESPYS • Justin Timberlake • Angelina Jolie • Puerto Rico • *familia* • J. Lo • New York Mets • Radiohead •
Raj style • *comida* • Daryl Hall and John Oates • Kate Hudson • Deee-Lite and Lady Miss Kier

Question 16

**"Who do
you usually
dress for?"**

*"I travel constantly
for work. My clothes
have to go from
airplane to meetings
to special events,
and all in one
carry-on suitcase."*

Bianca Gomez, 30

I'm the first person to say limit your wardrobe to neutrals if you travel, but when you do as much of it as Bianca does, it makes sense to develop a scheme that embraces color and surprise. Bianca's clothes have to go from meetings and luncheons to cocktail parties and even the red carpet for the annual ESPY awards.

A photograph of Bianca on her inspiration board says it all: She's standing in a doorway on a cobblestone street in Old San Juan, Puerto Rico, on vacation, wearing a Caribbean-hued T-shirt and jeans. Bianca says, "This picture represents who I am and my personality." How can this look of joy, of perfect style, translate into her work/travel wardrobe?

Spend money on well-made, quality pieces that will last and hold up to the rigors of travel. A two-piece suit and trench coat are classic, but consider alternatives that fit into your particular lifestyle. When going on a business trip, less is more. The less you can bring and yet still feel chic and amazing, the better. The more you can wear on the plane, so as to carry less luggage, even better.

On the plane, Bianca should wear jeans, an all-weather coat, a button-down shirt, and comfy shoes. Layer on a warm sweater and a big wrap too; they're cozy for sleeping on the plane. In her suitcase are a bright sheath dress and pumps for evenings, along with a dazzling pair of costume chandelier earrings (leave the good stuff at home when you travel). Flats, which have made a big fashion comeback, or moccasins take up far less room than heels, and for Bianca, who spends her days running around with a walkie-talkie, they're a lot more comfortable. One pair of heels is irresistible though! And check out the gorgeous orange ribbon dominating her inspiration board.

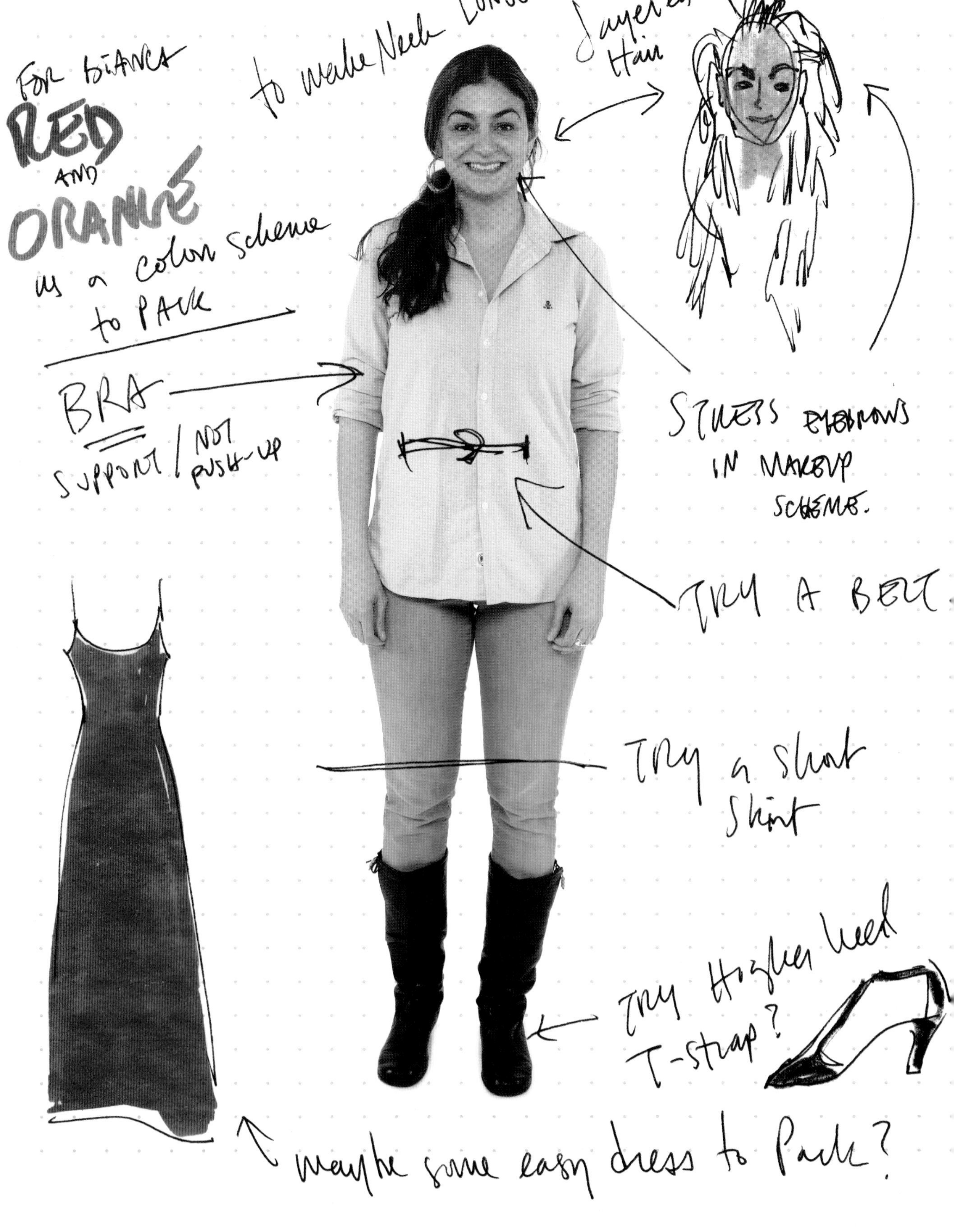

FOR BIANCA

RED AND ORANGE

as a color scheme to PACK

BRA
SUPPORT / NOT PUSH-UP

to make Neck LONGER:

Jayered Hair

STRESS EYEBROWS IN MAKEUP SCHEME.

TRY A BELT.

TRY a Short Skirt

TRY Higher Heel T-strap?

maybe some easy dress to Pack?

makeup: brow—perfect hair: getting to the roots

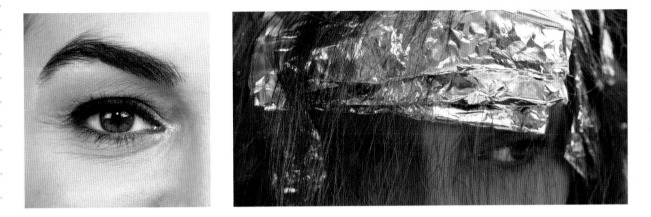

Look at the perfect shape of her brows. There are some random hairs here and there. Her brows look real! Bianca's brows are filled in with a brunet shade, brushed, and held in place with brow gel.

The pearly underbrow highlighter Bianca was wearing overpowered her eyes and made her look older. First concealer is applied to get rid of dark circles, then a sexy, smudgy, kohl-like look is achieved with thin black eyeliner, brown and navy shadows on the lids, and translucent powder underneath to brighten her eyes.

Bianca was concerned that making her hair darker would make her look older and very pale. ("Could we not go too dark?") Trust me, Bianca. First her hair was dyed to match her natural color, and then highlights were added, combing the color to the ends. The highlights brighten up Bianca's hair, and a trim adds lushness, bounce, and style.

Hair care on the go

While it's difficult to know how your hair is going to look and behave when you are traveling, here are some plan-ahead suggestions from Ryan.

- Check the weather. If you live in a dry climate, be prepared for the fact that hot, humid weather will make your hair curl. Literally.
- If your hotel stocks quality shampoos and conditioners like AVEDA or Neutrogena, for instance, you can trust them. Avoid two-in-one shampoo/conditioner products; they can strip the color from your hair and make it unruly. Pass on clear shampoos with a lot of artificial fragrances; they can be drying and damaging.
- Keep two sets of three-ounce bottles packed at the ready with your favorite hair products. Even if you check luggage, you don't want to take up precious space with lots of bottles.
- Travel with a treatment conditioner to bring life back to your hair. I recommend Crede, Kérastase, or Davines Nourishing Vegetarian Miracle.

- Hotel hair dryers are often too hot and bad for your hair. There are plenty of good portable dryers available that can be slipped into the corner of your suitcase.
- If you have a big meeting or a major event, ask the hotel's concierge to book an appointment for you at the best salon in town for a shampoo and blowout. Call before you arrive.

the plane truth

I never check a bag on airplanes, preferring to carry everything with me. My cashmere shawl is always with me. I travel with many bandanas; they are mood altering and don't take up much room. I often pack a pair or two of shoes. If the shoes are wrong, I will be miserable all day. Find the perfect balance of not packing too much, but still have options when you get to your destination.

A shawl, pashmina, big scarf, or sari wrap does double duty, keeping you warm on cold airplanes and in freezing meeting rooms as well as being a stylish wrap for all of your outfits.

Wear the most important and the most tailored items in your travel wardrobe—a suit, blazer, trench coat—on the plane and hang them up when you're not wearing them so you don't have to worry about wrinkled clothes when you arrive.

Flats and moccasins take up less room than heels, plus they make trekking from one end of an airport to the other much easier. Jazz, tap, and other dance shoes are also comfortable for travel.

It's true: Airline personnel are known to bump passengers from coach to first or business class on a filled plane if the passengers "look" as if they belong there, as awful as that fact is. Even more reason to dress well when traveling.

"Never skimp on toiletries when you travel. Home is where the toiletries are."

Dance shoes, like these open-toed heels, allow you to spend hours on your feet.

STEP 2: light up the night

Just as you build a look for traveling with a carry-on bag, also think about what goes into that bag for evening. Too often black is the fallback for evening, especially so when traveling. If you're going to wear black, that's fine. But gussy it up with immensely bright accessories.

Or, go all out with a colorful dress. The sleeves on the turquoise dress are too little-girly. Instead, Bianca's boho color sensibility is married with a versatile orange sheath for easy travel. By choosing your accessories and your evening outfit in the same family of colors, you won't worry about clashing or needing to pack more clothes.

> *Steady on your feet:*
> *How to walk in heels*
>
> When Bianca announced, "I don't know how to walk in high heels," I was like, "You what? Have you been living in a cave all of these years?" If I can do it, so can you. Stand tall; no slouching. Concentrate on putting the upper half of your body behind your waist and pushing your hips forward. Then walk. Commit to it.

the long and the short of it

Go into a dressing room and lift and lower skirt hems until you find the
right length for you. When trying to decide which shoes to wear with a skirt of
a particular length, the general rule is flats for long skirts, heels for short.
Try on everything to find the right hemline-shoe combo.

Are You Inspired?

"I am a woman obsessed. I am obsessed with playing back everything I learned from Isaac when I stare into my closet and think, 'I have nothing to wear.' I've given up that way of thinking. My usual stress of packing for business trips is gone, thanks to Isaac . . . and I approach travel feeling confident and put together. I am also obsessed with my trench coat and my orange cashmere hoodie. I wear them on every business trip, and I feel so stylish, professional, and comfortable. My orange cashmere hoodie is a comfy dream to wear on plane rides. I wear my big wrap for napping on the plane. This experience has turned around everything I used to think about traveling. Now I look forward to it."

ON THE PLANE

Layer on as much as you can. Wear jeans and moccasins for comfort.

• • •

ON THE GROUND

A quick change into your suit's trousers, a shirt, and a pair of heels.

• • •

Clap for her!

ON THE TOWN

Stand out in a sea of black.

...

Lisa's inspiration board

sailing the world • *Playbill* collection • King Tut • *The Gates* • Cyd Charisse • *The Band Wagon* •
Mickey Mouse • AFI's 100 Years . . . 100 Movies • costume jewelry

Question 22

"How do you think people see you style-wise?"

"I don't think they do, really. I'm just another mom in jeans. I just turned fifty, my oldest child left for college, and my mom just died. I've reached a point where I want to rediscover my own style. And everything is up for grabs."

Lisa Taylor, 50

You're fifty. (Or thirty or sixty or any number in between.) You can say, "I'm fifty. It's all downhill from here." Or defy the numbers and say, "I'm only fifty and I'm fabulous, stylish, and sexy. Why waste a single day looking less than spectacular? I'm fifty years old and I refuse to give up."

For many women like Lisa, as the years creep up, so do the pounds. You give up the gym, eat an unhealthy diet, and, before you know it, you're twenty pounds heavier than you were at forty. Twenty pounds unhappier. Losing parents and dealing with an empty nest add to the cycle of emotions and eating. Will you look back at those years and think, "I was fat/unhappy/in the wrong job or relationship. How did I allow this to happen?"

When it came to reconnecting with her former sense of style, Lisa found herself in a rut. A deep one. At six-foot-one, she knew finding pants and tops long enough for her legs and arms could be frustrating. Only one brand of jeans came with the necessary 35-inch inseam, so she relied on those for everything. And that means *every-*

thing—going to the theater, movies, or restaurants and meeting friends for lunch and shopping.

Lisa's inspiration board, however, exposed a glamour girl lurking beneath those jeans. She's seen all but three of the American Film Institute's top one hundred movies. The video box from *The Band Wagon*, with tall, long-legged Cyd Charisse, was on her board. It's Lisa's all-time favorite movie. There's a photo of her Playbill collection, with every play and musical she's ever seen. Travel photos of Lisa; her husband, Jonathan; son Russell; and daughter Avary on their sailboat filled her board. A touch of mink and some costume jewelry were also attached to the board.

Will you be like Lisa, who, after our first meeting, became inspired to focus on herself and reconnect with who she is by making some significant changes and choices? She went on a smart diet and lost weight. Worked out with a trainer at the gym. Redecorated her home.

Say hello to the new Lisa.

* UNCONSTRUCTED
JACKETS
TRY HIP LENGTH?

HAIR
NO
LONGER

EXTEND
EYES.
LINER?

HAIR: TALLER.
FULLER

* EMERGENCY
COLOR
CHECK !!!

* STRAIGHT-LEG
JEANS. NOT SO
FLARE
LEGGED
WHITE JEANS?

hair: S.O.S.

From all those days on her boat, Lisa's hair was sun-bleached, neglected, and sailing in
every direction. A stylish cut was crucial, but what about her color? Match her original color just
to cover up the gray, or try something new? A rich brunet color with a hint of auburn
brightens her face and matches her eyebrows.

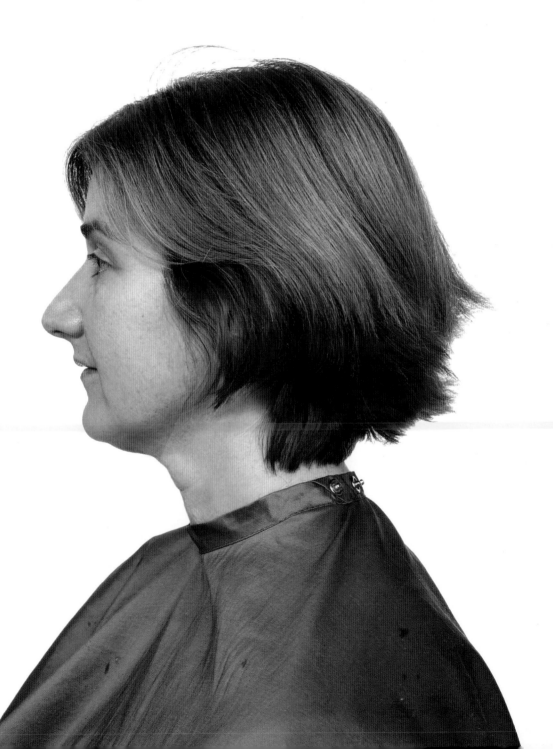

STEP 1:
white jeans

"I always steer away from white jeans, thinking they make me look fat."

Hardly. White jeans give Lisa a fresh look, play into her nautical life, and can be dressed up or down. These white Levi's have an easy-to-find 34-inch inseam, and Lisa can wear them ankle length since she's so tall (not that anyone's complaining about her long legs). Embracing this look makes it so much easier for her to find pants and jeans.

The jewel-encrusted jacket would be boring and mumsy-looking with black pants. A gray tank top in the same, rather than contrasting, color melts underneath the jacket, making the jacket the focus. White jeans make the outfit fresh, youthful, and glamorous.

An orange-and-pink striped Marimekko top flatters Lisa's coloring and is a modern take on the classic sailor shirt.

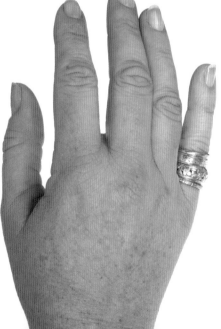

IT'S THE LITTLE THINGS

Lisa brought in a suitcase full of costume jewelry and treasures that belonged to her mother. Four generations of family-heirloom wedding rings stacked on her pinky finger became an instant classic. After a certain age, don't wear garish costume jewelry unless the pieces are high quality. Invest in some 18K gold or platinum jewelry with precious and semiprecious stones, and make them your everyday signature pieces. The chicest way to wear your jewelry is in a throwaway way.

"It's possible to lose weight without going on a diet. Simply pay attention to what you eat and eat less. It takes longer to drop the pounds, but they stay off for good."

Go on a diet. A little one.

"What's your least favorite body part?"

"My middle—too much belly fat. And who stole my waist?"

Don't like how those jeans fit anymore? Or how you can't quite close the zipper on your favorite skirt? If you don't like what you see in the mirror, then go on a short, sensible diet. Eat less, exercise more, and you will lose five, eight, or ten—I'm not talking about a lot of weight—pounds. It's not that hard, and you'll look better in a matter of weeks.

I can tell you from personal experience that losing a small amount of weight is so much easier than having to lose twenty-five or fifty pounds. About six months before I turned thirty, I decided that I no longer wanted to be fat. I said to myself, "You are fat now. You are going to be thirty. Will you look back at your thirties and say, 'What on earth was I thinking? How could I have sacrificed what is supposed to be the sexiest time of my life, the prime of my life, being fat?'"

It was time to stop rationalizing and making excuses. ("Okay, darling, you had a tough day. You deserve a few of those cookies.") That approach no longer worked for me. It was time to do a 180-degree turn and do the opposite: Stop trying. I just had to do it. And I did. So did Lisa. So can you.

"I made some basic shifts in my eating patterns. When I'm on a losing streak, I just eat less, say one half sandwich for lunch instead of a whole one. When I'm holding steady and evaluating, I allow myself the whole sandwich. This shifting back and forth seems to work for me," reports Lisa.

Lose ten pounds for fun. Starting is the hardest part. Once you make a little progress, you get into it and it's fun.

STEP 2: for me?

"I never thought I could wear a dress like this!"
And why not? It's simple, beautifully cut, and age
appropriate. And you never know until you try it
on. What's the worst thing that can happen? It
goes back on the rack.

When Lisa put on this dress, she immediately
felt amazing in it. How amazing? Reinvented.
Renewed. Reinspired.

choosing jewelry

Nope, no choker for Lisa.
It looks matronly on a woman
of her age. A bare neck and
décolletage are much pre-
ferred, but that doesn't mean
attention shouldn't be brought
to her face. Substantial diamond cocktail earrings, not
precious studs, make a statement with a dress like this.

"Style is 95 percent confidence (and 30 percent accessories)."

I told you so!

CASUAL LOUNGING

With her tall, regal frame,
Lisa can wear a sophisticated caftan without its
overwhelming her.

• • •

ASHORE

A barn coat updated with
heavy hardware has a twist of elegance and glam
that works on or off the boat.

• • •

Are You Inspired?

"Isaac gave me a wake-up call and reminded me that I count. After years of being a mommy and caring for aging parents,
I learned that I am important, too. I bought myself a year of Pilates and personal training, telling everyone that this is the Year of Lisa! As I sit here
in my extra-tall size 8 jeans, I feel confident and stylish for the first time in ages. (Was I wearing size 12 or 14 jeans at our first meeting?)
I spend more time on me, my clothes, my hair, my makeup, and my fitness regimen, so I feel better about everything in my life and the world looks
completely different. The happy ending to my chapter is that I discovered
how to look and feel great at fifty!"

ABOVE DECK

Gray jeweled jacket becomes
supercasual when worn with gold sandals
and a silver handbag.

• • •

THE DRESS OF HER DREAMS

Shapely and age appropriate; this dress is youthful
but not immature. And the purple color is one Lisa would have
never considered before.

• • •

Brooke's inspiration board

Ellen DeGeneres • black, white, and pink • Madonna • John Currin • Breck girl • Audrey Hepburn • Xanadu •
peonies • Scrabble • Peyton and Caroline • beach • Barbie dolls

Question 11

"What's your biggest style challenge?"

"I'm a stay-at-home mom who never seems to be at home. I wear jeans from morning to night. From the playground to the Smithsonian to ballet practice, my daughters and I are always on the go. To strike a balance, I have date nights out with my husband, Andrew, and girls' nights out with my friends. It's on these evenings that I feel a bit stuck and out of touch style-wise."

Brooke Fern, 34

From her inspiration board, we can tell that like many women, Brooke is eclectic. She is inspired by a variety of influences. Brooke loves clean lines, monograms, Scrabble, and the beach. She collects *Rolling Stone* covers, loves Madonna, and is a fan of contemporary figurative painter John Currin's work. Isn't it fabulous that she has such varied interests? What a great place to start.

Once Brooke puts on her "mommy-form" jeans, she has no time to change during the day. Brooke was reluctant to give up her jeans, so I urged her to embrace them. Why not wear denim all the time? Brooke can build a signature style around those jeans. How? By treating her jeans and other denim pieces—shirts, jackets, skirts—like building blocks that can support whatever else is layered on. And with a stash of accessories that turn her daytime jeans into something fabulous for night.

I mean wearing denim in inspired ways.

Hey, listen, it's so important that you start with the right jeans. Once you have jeans that fit and look fabulous, don't stop there. If you want to be into denim, then be into denim. The key to making a denim lifestyle work is the surprise of the shoes, handbags, scarves, belts, costume jewelry, and headbands that you wear with it.

Don't be afraid of denim. Pile it on. You'd wear a black T-shirt and black jacket together, so why not a denim shirt and denim jacket?

And unlock that inner shoe obsession. If you're going to wear flip-flops, then make them fabulous and colorful. Try jeweled or animal-print flats or, even better, three-inch heels for evening.

Brooke doesn't have to give up her denim. Just find new ways to embrace it.

JEAN JACKET.

BROOKE'S EYES ARE SUBTLY DOWN-TURNED CAN WE EMPHASIZE CORNERS? FALSE EYELASHES? MASCARA?

HIPPIE SANDALS

RUGATI BAG WOULD SOLVE ALL HER PROBLEMS. * MAYBE IN HER FAVORITE COLOR?

makeup: embrace those freckles

First thing I said to Brooke was, "Stop covering up those gorgeous freckles with foundation!" Now, this is a perfect example of someone trying to hide what she perceives as a flaw. Nothing is more aging than a layer of foundation; avoid using it. Instead, just a tad of concealer to cover the redness on her chin and sides of her nose.

A couple tricks make Brooke's eyes look larger and brighter. First, concealer is applied under her eyes. Always use your ring finger to blend for the lightest touch.

Since Brooke's eyes droop at the outer edges, her false eyelashes open up her eyes and are trimmed more than usual to avoid bringing down her eyes even more. (See page 145 for applying false eyelashes.) No time for false eyelashes? Use an eyelash curler, followed by two coats of mascara to hold the curl.

A dark taupe powder is applied to her eyelids to give the illusion of a crease and to create depth. A lightening wand is applied to the inner corners of the eyelids for a bright, wide-opened look.

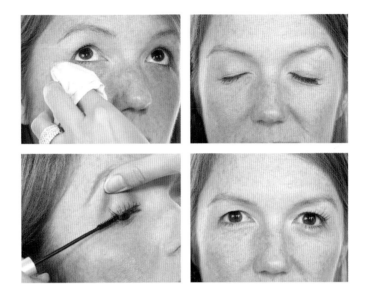

hair: hey, red!

Thick, lush, and red, but too thick to be manageable. Once cut, thinned, and layered, Brooke's hair has body and shape, and it can be worn loose or up in a ponytail. Her hair was good. Now it's great.

STEP 1: buying the right jeans

Don't buy jeans with fake striping and faux weathering and washes past a certain age (fourteen); they look cheap and are unflattering. A change in the color of the denim down the leg breaks up the clean line and tends to shorten the leg or enhance curves where you don't want them.

A pair of jeans should feel as if they were made specifically for you and molded to your body. Sit and walk in them to make sure the fit is right. Buy a pair of clean dark-wash classic jeans and take good care of them by dry-cleaning or washing them, inside out, in cold water. Hang them to dry; never put your jeans in the dryer. Brooke is wearing unwashed denim A.P.C. jeans.

When I was a kid, jeans were worn only during weekends or when cleaning out the garage. Jeans have become a cultural phenomenon; we wear them all the time and for any occasion.

There are as many considerations when wearing jeans as there are about dressing for a black-tie formal. Trouser-fit or low-rise jeans. Color and wash. The length. These details can make or break the effect you're after. Some woman love a hem that scrapes the floor, while others find that look sloppy and prefer shorter jeans. Ask yourself what image you want to get across when wearing jeans.

STEP 2: building blocks

Once you have the perfect jeans, start building your outfit by layering with more denim. Perhaps a denim jacket or vest over a denim shirt. Then try different hues of one particular color. A skirt instead of jeans. Heeled sandals instead of flat ones. Keep going, and keep looking.

Use the same color down to the tiniest details, like this wristload of costume bracelets in every shade of blue to go with Brooke's top and scarf.

flower power

The denim jacket stays, but the T-shirts are replaced with a denim shirt, and a flower skirt replaces the jeans. The look is still very much a denim statement. Red handbag and a "mom" bag for all of Brooke's stuff. Red flats? Red heels? They both work.

"Multitask denim. It works for you in more than one way."

STEP 3: gold medal

Brooke doesn't have a lot of time to change her clothes, so when she wants to dress up, all she has to do is slip on this gold pleated skirt, buckle on a big belt, slip into some heels, and grab her gold evening bag.

*Here are some
other ways
to dress up denim*

- *Metallic jacket*
- *Fur or faux fur*
- *Designer handbag*
- *Crisp white blouse*
- *Bejeweled flats*
- *Glittery jacket*
- *Your best jewelry*
- *Glamorous sunglasses*
- *Eye-catching belt*
- *Satin or sequins*

What a knockout!

DRESS IT UP

Amazing how this look comes together when metallic fabrics are paired with denim.

• • •

Are You Inspired?

"Gosh, was I lazy. It was way too easy to throw on my jeans and go. I learned it's just as easy to put some thought into how I look. And definitely more fun. I wear more color and more heels with denim. Isaac made me understand that there is a reason to put effort into the way I look every day. I wouldn't invite people over for dinner and not clean my house first: It's the same with getting dressed in the morning. Even if I'm spending the day at the playground with my daughters, I should look good doing it. I'm grateful for that lesson. I'm so much more open to things that I never would have considered before. Having my own style is just as easy as having no style . . . . So why wouldn't I do that?"

AM I BLUE?

Denim is a fabric *and* a shade of blue.
Once you choose a color, go for multiple tones.

• • •

DAYTRIPPING

Comfy and layered; perfect for a day
at the park or the zoo.

• • •

Mary Kate's inspiration board

Dita Von Teese • Paris opera • *Six Feet Under* • Deborah Harry • pink chrysanthemum • *Rear Window* • fleur de lys • Dior's New Look •
Plan de Paris • Princess Leia • *Soir Bleu* by Edward Hopper • David Bowie • *Moulin Rouge*

Question 21

"**What look or style
have you always
wanted to try but
have never had
the nerve?**"

"*Femme fatale.*"

Mary Kate Gaudet, 26

There's something I need to get off my chest. Every girl I've ever met, skinny, large, or average, thinks she's fat. I have rarely met a girl whose appearance matches her self-perception. No one is comfortable in her own skin. Ironically, to me, most of the time she looks just right. Of course, losing five pounds always makes us feel better, and it's probably healthier, but that doesn't really answer the style question. The question shouldn't be "How can I look skinny when I'm really not?" The question should be, "How can I be stylish with my large figure?"

It's just like plastic surgery. It might make you feel a little better to have a face-lift, but it doesn't make you look younger. You're not fooling anyone.

The thing that drew me and my team to Mary Kate was that she didn't ask us to make her look thinner; she asked us to make her feel sexier. As soon as I saw her inspiration board, I said, "This girl has style and knows what she likes!" Smack in the center was pinup star and burlesque performer Dita Von Teese, who I adore. And the colors Mary Kate loves—red, black, and purple—were everywhere. Her inspiration board screamed agent provocateur–film noir–French *Vogue* mademoiselle.

Learning how to have style is all about learning to express yourself. It requires an I-deserve-it attitude and plenty of self-confidence. Mary Kate has both. Her eyes lit up when I suggested the idea of sexy undergarments and a 1930s Hollywood hairdo for her inner vixen, with a more subdued look for the workday.

So what was holding her back? Convention. Well, if there's one thing I don't like, it's convention of any kind. Mary Kate is a woman with her own innate, quirky sense of style no matter what size she wears. Together, we tried to shatter convention: The idea that you have to be thin to be sexy. Who wrote these rules? It took self-control on my part not to recommend that Mary Kate lose weight, and it took bravery on her part to go for this makeover, but I think we both succeeded. What is style if not bravery?

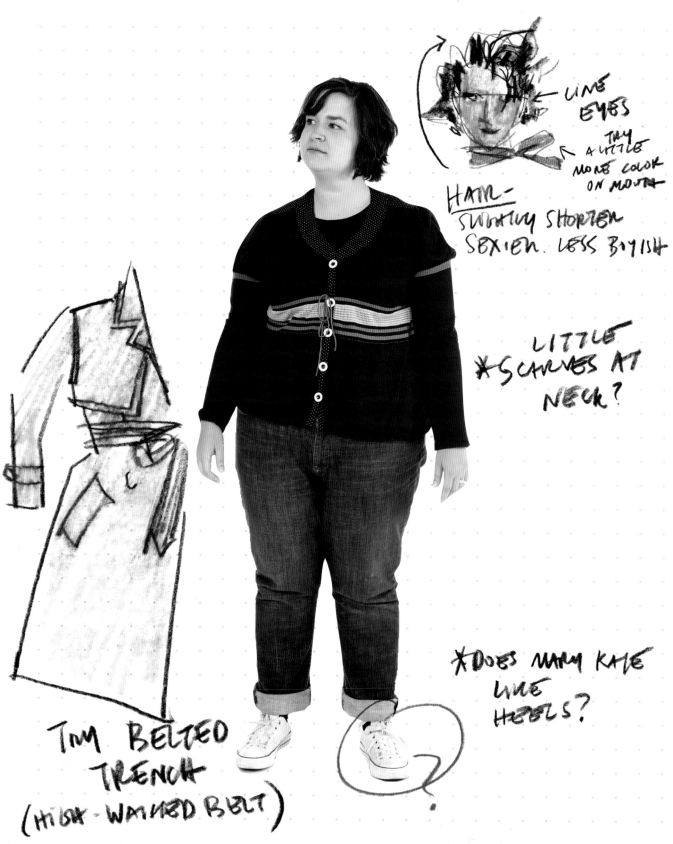

LINE EYES

TRY A LITTLE MORE COLOR ON MOUTH

HAIR—
SLIGHTLY SHORTER
SEXIER. LESS BOYISH

LITTLE
*SCARVES AT
NECK?

TINY BELTED
TRENCH
(HIGH-WAISTED BELT)

*DOES MARY KATE
LIKE
HEELS?

When lining the top lid, don't draw the line
all the way to the edge of the eye,

but pull it up just before the end.
The thicker the eyeliner, the more dangerous
the woman.

A matte taupe shadow gives definition to the creases
on Mary Kate's eyes. No mascara on the lower lashes, just
a smudge of taupe eye shadow. A soft fuchsia lip color
brings brightness to a black wardrobe. Mary Kate's skin is
flawless—just a bit of powder foundation
applied with a brush.

hair: crop shop

I wanted to see Mary Kate's hair short in the back, so it was chopped off.
And again. And again. Sometimes you just have to keep at it until the final version is what
you want. Don't be afraid to ask the same of any hairstylist.

STEP 1:
opportunity knocks

Listen, I know what happens—it's Monday morning and you are feeling fat. You reach for that same pair of black pants and black sweater because you think it will hide your figure and deflect attention. Don't think I'm not guilty of falling into this trap, wearing the same look over and over again. You can ask anyone in my office. But once I switch it up, almost everyone I come in contact with comments on how great I look. Plus, I feel remarkably better. Isn't that what it's all about?

Even if it's nothing more than the right pair of better-fitting jeans. These have a dark blue wash and are tailored and tapered through the legs. Mary Kate's blouse features reds and purples from her inspiration board. Navy or black footwear and bag would be predictably boring. Cognac brown high-heeled oxfords with a vintage feel and a satchel bag dress up her look.

how to tie a scarf

What French woman doesn't wear a scarf? Fold a scarf lengthwise until it is
the desired width. Hold two-thirds of the scarf in one hand and the rest in the other. Wrap
the long part around the back of your neck so the short part of the scarf meets in front
of your neck. Make a simple knot in the front—over and under—and then tighten it a bit.
Et voilà! See how Mary Kate's colored neck scarves bring attention to her face?

STEP 2:

underneath it all

Today's comfortable, lightweight undergarments help hide troublesome figure problems somewhat while lending a longer, leaner line to your silhouette. Body shapers by Spanx are available in many styles to shape your butt, tuck in your tummy, or emphasize your waist. Tummy Tuck Jeans give your tush a lift and flatten your belly.

Are You Inspired?

"I'm inspired to be more put together. I've gotten away with looking cool and stylish, but I'm a grown-up now, and there are ways I can upgrade my look without losing my personality. Accessories. Color. Shoes. Oh, and tailoring! It's amazing what a little investment in your clothing can do. The smallest snips make the biggest differences. Spending an extra five minutes putting together ensembles, 'instead of just getting dressed,' and using my makeup brushes make me feel like a million bucks. I had sort of given up on myself, and Isaac gave me the jump-start that I needed. I feel sexy."

MADE FOR MYSTERY

Belted coat defines her waist.
Seams up the back of tights are sexy in
a French kind of way.

• • •

STYLE THAT SHINES

Nighttime doesn't always mean
wearing all black.

• • •

Voilà!

Lara's inspiration board

Water Lilies by Claude Monet • blueberries • "They *hated* to spread gossip" • London • platform heels • Martha's Vineyard •
flowing dresses • Paris • "Frugal is *such an ugly* word" • peonies and rhododendrons • big handbags

Question 1

**What colors
do you wear most
frequently?**

*"I often wear just
black slacks and
a button-down shirt
or a black dress.
I'm constantly
figuring out how
to look work
appropriate without
looking frumpy.
I just don't have any
originality or color
in my wardrobe."*

Lara Hall, 31

If anyone understands where Lara is coming from, it's me. As much as I fill my world and my work with color, I frequently wear black. It's slimming. It's easy. It's always appropriate.

Well, Lara, just because you work in the corporate world doesn't mean you have to wear only black. In fact, in some corporate environments black is frowned upon as severe and unfriendly. Sure, black pieces—the little black dress, black cashmere sweater, black heels—are important building blocks in every woman's wardrobe. But wearing all black, all the time, makes a girl dull. You are doing nothing to stand out from the crowd.

On her questionnaire, Lara said that her number one color is turquoise and her favorite painting is "any of Monet's *Water Lilies*. I love to visit the ones at the Museum of Modern Art because the room is so filled with light and color."

Talk about having sources of inspiration for getting color into your wardrobe! Lara's board features tons of blue—blue sky, blueberries, blue water—and pink and red—peonies, rhododendrons, and painted furniture.

Don't be afraid of colors. Experiment with them. Just as you have to try on a lot of clothes to find the shapes that are perfect for you, you have to try on clothes in lots of different colors too. Play with colors that you think might clash. Remember how your mother told you never to wear orange and pink together? She was so wrong. That's one of my favorite combinations. Consider wearing all one color or several shades of a particular hue from top to bottom. Use accessories for extra color.

Like Monet, make an impression. Invite more color into your life.

CONSIDER
BLEACHING
HAIR

GREEN
DRESS

TURQUOISE
SHOE

(TALLER OR
FLATER HEELS!)

TONALITY

PINK SUIT
PALE PINK
BLOUSE
BURGUNDY SHOE

ETC......

hair: how blonde will you go?

Lara reminds me—her coloring and her features—of a cousin of mine who has been a platinum blonde for years. When I suggested to Lara that she become a blonder blonde, there was no hesitation. "Go for it." Sometimes style is all about bravery. Turn the page.

bombshell

Lara becomes a stunning blonde
à la Kim Novak and Gwen
Stefani. For evening, her hair
was finger-waved. It may
be too extreme for every day,
but worth it for a special
occasion.

color theory

Take small steps when first adding color. It's fine to wear neutrals; check out this checked suit. Accessorize with one color in a bunch of different hues. Like these pink accessories—shirt, scarf, shoes, handbag, and lipstick— in a variety of shades.

Scarf trick

A scarf is the easiest way to add color to a ho-hum outfit. You can mix patterns and textures. A daytime outfit becomes instantly nighttime chic with a scarf, especially when traveling. Scarves take up so little space; shove a few into the corner of your suitcase.

By the way, pink is not the only

color you can do this with . . .

STEP 2:

color theory

Once you've embraced colors, start mixing them within spectrums. Pair different shades of one color—like this dark blue satiny dress with turquoise satin wedge sandals.

"Color is the greatest luxury of all. You don't buy color the way you buy black or beige. It's a special day when you buy pink or jade green."

Try adding color with shoes and other accessories. Look how this turquoise satin ankle wedge becomes a staple shoe for Lara. Who would have ever thought they'd be as basic as a black pump?

out
of the blue

JUST LOOKING

Think of these jeans just like
a pair of regular jeans or black pants.
Except they're turquoise. Almost any
top goes with them.

Contrary to the idea that turquoise should also be in the
top, choose a complementary color instead to avoid a too-matched look.
And see how black is quietly added back in.

Right on!

DECLARE NEUTRALITY

No need to stay away from all neutrals—
including white.

•••

Are You Inspired?

"When shopping now, I've become very conscious of buying something in a color rather than just black. I bought a gorgeous blue dress and a bunch of bright sweaters in orange, pink, and burgundy. They're so pretty! My platinum-blonde hair has changed my life! It definitely attracts a lot of attention from guys. Cowboys in particular like platinum blondes! My hair gets me noticed at the office too. Now the president of our company knows who I am and says hello whenever I pass him in the hall. It can be hard to stand out in a company of 65,000 employees! What is better than that? I'm a whole new Lara Hall!"

LIVING GREEN

Matching accessories would be a huge mistake here.
Imagine all black shoes and bag. Yuck.

• • •

ROYAL BLUE

Instead of a black dress, pick a color.
Then add another color with the shoes. And another.
And another.

• • •

Susan's inspiration board

patterns and prints • Little Miss Drama • diamonds • the horizon • Lucy Liu • hearts and flowers • red, pink, and purple •
midcentury modern • *The Secret* • black heels and opaque tights

"What's the one item
in your closet that
you wear again and
again and again?"

*"Nothing. My friends
tell me that they
never see me wear
the same thing twice.
My closets are
crammed with clothes
barely or never worn.
Plastic containers
stuffed with shoes,
boots, bags, belts,
and scarves are under
the bed. I still have
nothing to wear.
I have hundreds of
pieces, but no outfits,
and nothing seems
to go together."*

Susan Claxton, 38

Susan shopped too much. Way too much. She shopped every day! The salespeople in the discount stores and outlets she frequents know her by name. Susan's even online-friendly with a saleswoman at a discount handbag store in Tennessee, who e-mails her a daily inventory list. Most of Susan's items were bought on sale and still had tags on them. Lots of her pieces didn't even fit because she lost forty pounds and she didn't shop by her new size. And she found it impossible to part with anything.

But, wait, there was a silver lining to all of her stuff! Among all her things were some great, stylish pieces. She has an amazing, eclectic eye. But, although drawn to patterns and prints, Susan was too timid to mix and match them for a unique look

It was time for fashion triage. Kristen and I went through racks upon racks of her clothes, bins of shoes, and bags of handbags and had Susan make a huge pile of stuff to give to charity. We got rid of clothes that were too big; clothes bought on sale and never worn; worn-out clothes; waiting-to-be-repaired shoes that would never make it to the shoemaker; and screamingly dated things.

My goals were to teach Susan how to shop well by shopping less and how to combine the colors and patterns in her closet. Buying better-quality clothes and work-horse accessories may cost more money, but they will last for years. I wanted Susan to learn how to be a "collector" rather than just an overshopper, an elemental imperative for every woman.

When it comes to buying clothes, think like an art collector who buys paintings from a particular period or artist. Collectors become intimately knowledgeable about their areas of expertise. They visit galleries and auction houses to study paintings. If a specific work is appealing, they ask for a photograph or transparency so they can study it. Sometimes they buy a painting; other times they miss out on a purchase because it's been sold to another collector. But that's okay. Whether it's midcentury art, first-edition books, or Bordeaux wines, all collectors have one thing in common: They don't buy everything they see. That goes for clothes and accessories too.

Susan had to learn the difference between impulse buying and thoughtful collecting.

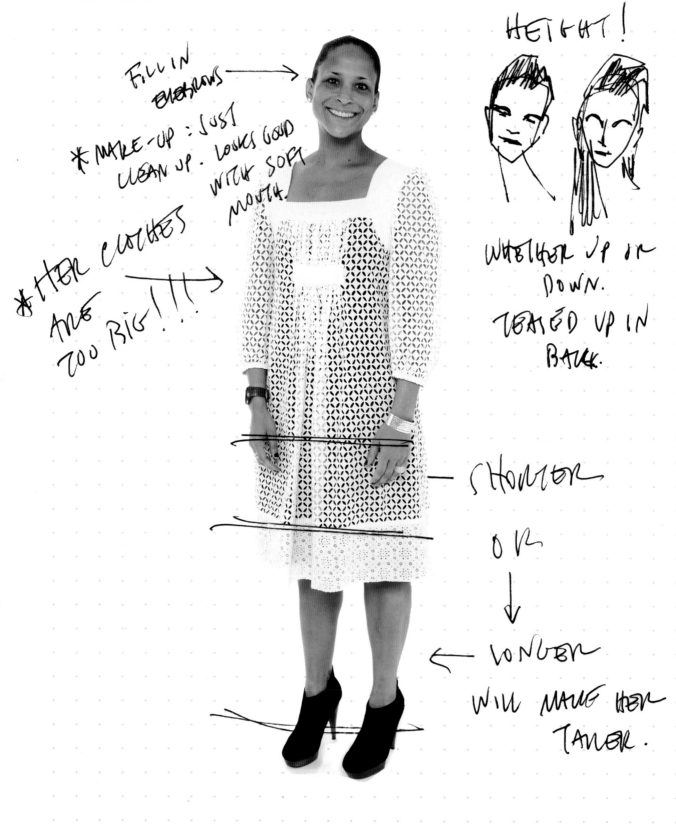

FILL IN EYEBROWS

* MAKE-UP : JUST CLEAN UP. LOOKS GOOD WITH SOFT MOUTH.

* HER CLOTHES ARE TOO BIG !!!

HEIGHT!

WHETHER UP OR DOWN. TEASED UP IN BACK.

— SHORTER

OR

↓

← LONGER

WILL MAKE HER TALLER.

Tags, tags, and more tags on Susan's unworn, on-sale clothes.

the closet

When Susan came in with her inspiration board, she proudly wore a dress bought on sale—just as she buys all of her clothes. It was love at first sight for the lacy, creamy, peek-a-boo dress worn over a slip. Susan "visited" her dress in the store almost daily for three months, and when the price dropped from $350 to $85, she bought it.

One thing: It was no longer available in her size, so she bought it one size larger. Since the underslip was missing, she negotiated on the price. Some bargain.

Susan should have paid full price for the right-size dress. In the summer, she could wear it with a camisole, ankle-length tights, and sandals; in the winter, with a full-length bodysuit and boots. Instead, she's stuck with a dress that's way too big, can't be altered, and is just completely wrong for her.

Since it was so hard to imagine all her clothes and accessories, I went to her apartment with a photographer. There were plenty of great things, packed in with stuff she never wore.

Why does Susan keep buying all of this stuff? No one needs to go shopping every day. Susan has to start looking at her clothes as an investment, not as a game where she bids on pieces at the lowest price.

Ask yourself, "What am I worth?"

There was only one way to decide what Susan should keep and what she should discard: Bring every single outfit, dress, and pair of shoes from her closets, bins, and bags to the studio and try them all on. She did. Wow, did this girl have stuff!

Your look book

Ever look through your closet and you wonder, "Hmmm, would that black skirt go with my new red sweater and those ankle boots?" You try it on and realize that you have created a great-looking new outfit.

Take this idea one step further, and put together what is known in the fashion industry as a "look book." Every season, designers produce a book with photographs showing the new looks in that season's collection.

Now Susan puts her digital camera on top of her television and takes pictures of herself in outfits before going out. She downloads the images to her computer and refers to her look book to remember what jewelry, shoes, and other accessories she wore with a particular outfit. Knowing what goes together saves time, so there's no last-minute rush figuring out which shoes go with which pants. Also, Susan believes that photos give a truer picture of how good (or bad) she looks than looking in a mirror. That's so true.

Make it fun! Spend a weekend afternoon trying on and mixing and matching clothes, and take photographs of yourself in each one. Put together a gazillion outfits from workday to wacky and see what works. What are the craziest things you can put together? What's the outfit that seems so "not you"? Those days of staring at your closet for fifteen minutes every morning will be over.

If an outfit works, great! If not, get rid of it.

"To have style, there must be an emotional and physical connection and passion to the clothes you buy and own."

SHOES

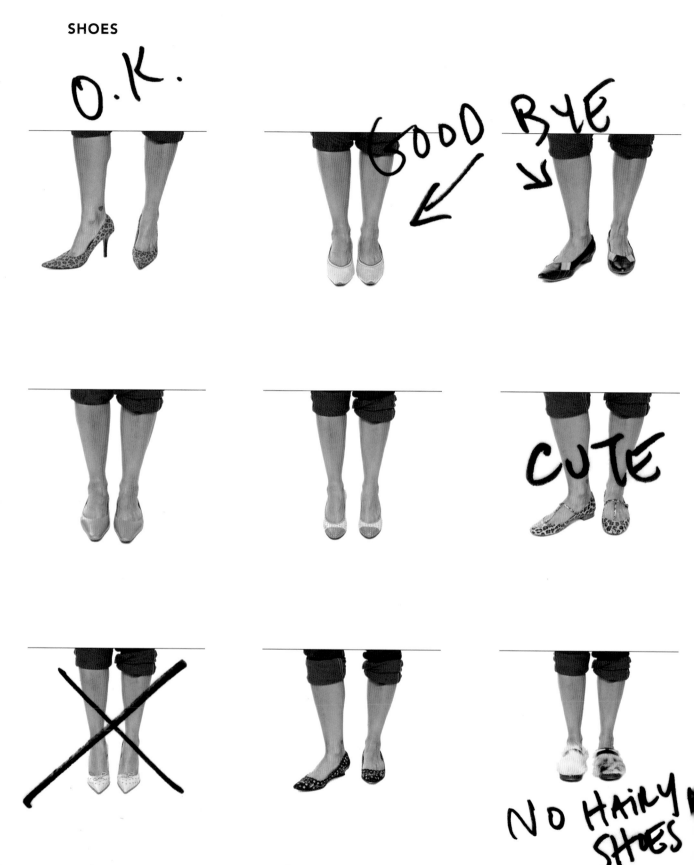

O.K.

GOOD BYE

CUTE

NO HAIRY SHOES

"Before making a purchase, ask yourself, 'Why do I want to buy this? Is this a must-have item that will round out my wardrobe? Will I feel great wearing it?' What's the point of owning things if they don't make you feel good?"

STEP 2:

mixing prints and patterns

Susan has a great sense of color and a unique eclecticism when it comes to clothes. When putting prints and patterns together, be brave, follow these guidelines, and ask yourself, "Does the mix feel right?" Remember, there's a fine line between mixing patterns successfully and not.

- Coordinate separates so one color repeats in all of the pieces. This is not to be confused with matching . . . that's the last thing in the world you want to do.
- Pair structured, repeating patterns (polka dots) with loose ones (swirls).
- Combine small prints and patterns (herringbones) with larger ones (big florals).

STEP 3:

anchor your
prints

Almost anything can be anchored with a black turtleneck,
black tights, and black shoes. Look what happened when Susan did just
that with a bunch of dresses.

"One woman's 'too much' is another woman's 'basic black.'"

Shopping versus buying

When we first met, Susan made a promise to herself and to me not to buy anything for one month. She lasted three days.

Sound familiar?

Susan has to love, appreciate, adore, flip over, cherish, and worship every item in her wardrobe. She has to stop buying, but not stop shopping.

Go to stores and look, but don't look at price tags and don't buy a thing. (Leave your credit cards home too.) Go to a store's or designer's website and download photos. Pick up a bunch of fashion magazines, and clip photos and ads that speak to you. Spread your images out and study them while shopping in your closet: "Which of these items do I already own? Would that navy blazer in my closet look better if it had three-quarter sleeves? What do I need more this year—a new bag or a new cashmere cardigan?"

Once you decide that a new handbag is really what you need, go for it, even if you find yourself saying that designer bag is way too expensive.

Well, it's not, and here's why: If you, like Susan, didn't buy ten things at $40, you'd have $400 toward that coveted bag in no time. That name-brand bag will last for years and look fabulous. You worked hard for it. You deserve it. You are worth it.

The inexpensive skirt, sweater, and coat are all from Susan's closets. The Fendi bag and Christian Louboutin mules are modern and chic.

STEP 4:

know when to go over the top

If you're going to mix prints and patterns, then anchor the look with to-die-for shoes. Hmmm, something was missing . . . how about a crinoline? It takes nerve to wear one, but this is the outfit to do it with.

I love it!

STRIPES AND DOTS

Polka-dot tights pick up the pink in Susan's
own sweater dress. Black accessories and coat pull the
whole look together.

•••

ANIMAL INSTINCTS

Yes, you can mix animal prints with other patterns.
It's a jungle out there.

•••

Are You Inspired?

"You know, it's funny, when I first met Isaac, I was feeling pretty confident about the way I looked every day. I was shocked that I could learn so much, that I was getting so much wrong. It's like anything, you get into a pattern and you go with it. I'm thrilled that I've learned a new pattern. I am now fearless when it comes to mixing and matching patterns. I don't need any more new clothes from the stores I used to shop at, but I try to stay focused on finding great-quality pieces in vintage stores that work with what I already have. I'm becoming a collector of my own style!"

SMALL, MEDIUM, AND LARGE

Remember the small, medium, large
rule when mixing patterns: Small zebra print, medium chain
pattern, and large plaid.

• • •

VINTAGE ECLECTIC

Big necklaces pick up the colors in
a Lanvin thrift-store find.

• • •

Keri's inspiration board

Sarah Silverman • "I Love New York" • Richard Simmons • Amy Winehouse • Philip Roth •
Mary-Kate and Ashley Olsen • Andy Samberg • America Ferrara

Question 23

**"What's the one
thing you'd like to
tell the world?"**

*"Have more fun.
You only live once."*

Keri Keane, 30

The first thing I thought when I met Keri was, "Boy, she's funny! And sexy."

It used to be that the funny girls were the ones who couldn't get dates. But now they're having the last laugh. Funny is the new sexy. Sarah Silverman is funny and sexy. Margaret Cho is funny and sexy. Tina Fey is funny and sexy. Amy Poehler is funny and sexy. Sometimes we hide sexiness behind being funny. Do I need to continue?

Keri knew she was funny, but she was hiding her sexiness by dressing like a seventeen-year-old, wearing ill-fitting sweatshirts, T-shirts, and jeans for going out. The colors—black, white, and gray—she favored were about as sexy as prison stripes. Yet there was something delightful and charming about that look that was worth keeping—her vigor and her enthusiasm came through loud and clear.

But wait! Look at her inspiration board—she looks amazing in the lower right photo, wearing black lace and showing some cleavage! Talk about sexy.

Keri loves live music, trashy reality shows, New York City, beer, cotton candy, checking things off lists, folding laundry, the smell of chlorine, her iPod, and having her arms tickled. And her dancing eyes and mischievous smile say, "I'm a woman who knows how to have a good time."

Keri knew she was in a fashion rut. "I hate getting dressed for work in the morning; I feel like I'm wearing a uniform. Every day, it's sweater and pants or sweater and skirt. People often mistake me for an intern."

Keri needed to lighten up her style in every way. Bring out her eyes with the right makeup. Put on some lipstick to make that grin even more attractive. Find casual and work clothes that fit and are in a bright color palette. For going out, release the kooky fashion diva within.

Funny + Sexy = Keri.

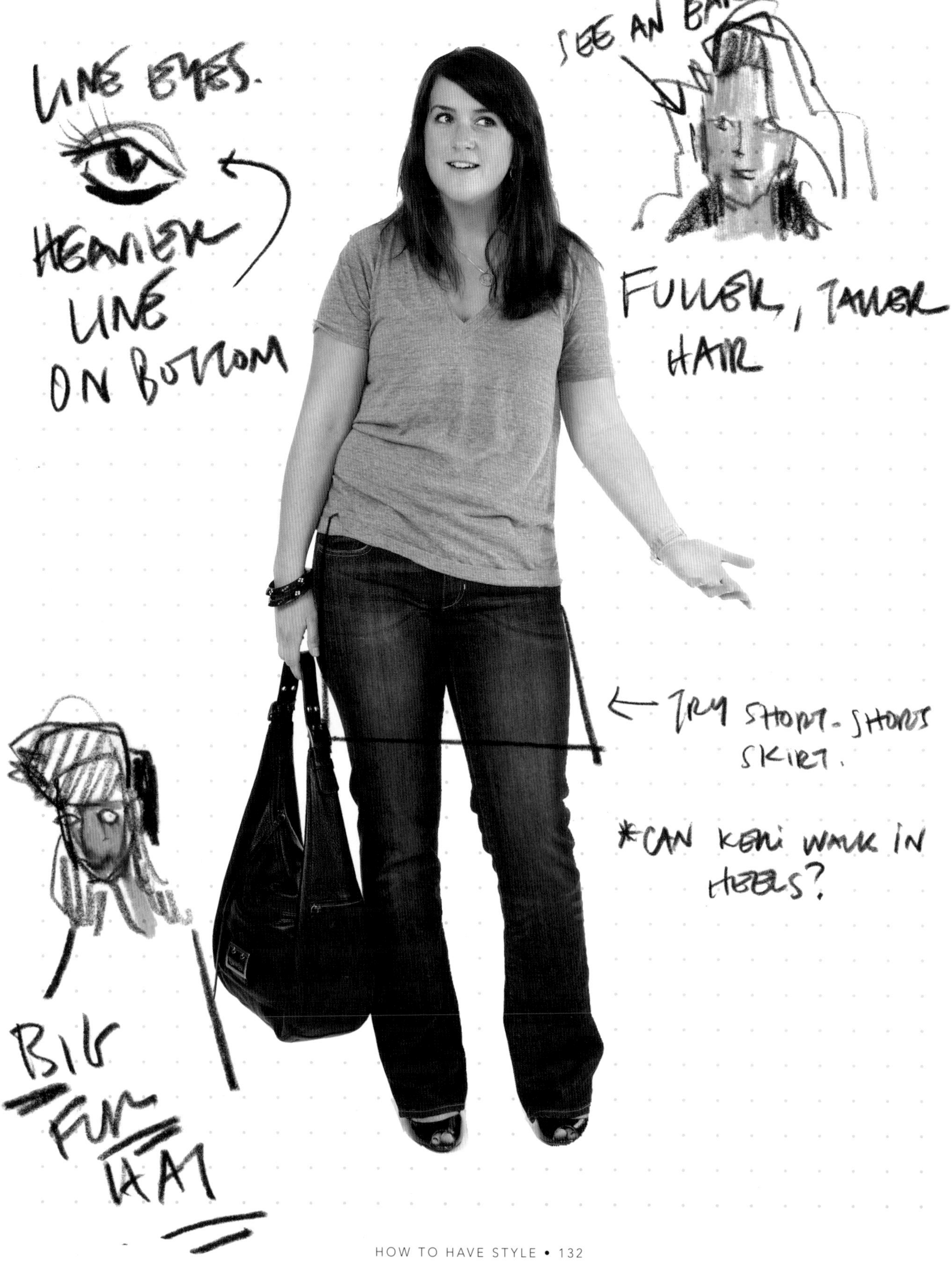

LINE EYES.

HEAVIER LINE ON BOTTOM

SEE AN EAR

FULLER, TALLER HAIR

← TRY SHORT-SHORTS SKIRT.

*CAN KERI WALK IN HEELS?

BIG FUN HAT

Keri expresses herself down to her toes.

hair: swoop and swirl

Just a trim, some swooping curls, and a sexy sweep of hair falling over one eye.

Eyebrows

Hey, listen to me, everybody: Stop tweezing your eyebrows so much! Keri, Lisa, and Regan couldn't believe it when I asked them to let their eyebrows grow in for two months! The era of the skinny, skinny eyebrow is over. You can be sure that fuller eyebrows will be the style for the next ten years.

Forget all that plucking. Throw off the perfection a bit.

Sure, it's fine to get rid of some stray hairs, but not all of them. Eyebrows should provide a distinctive frame for the rest of your face and shouldn't be too thick, too thin, or too perfect. Once your eyebrows grow in, have them tweezed or threaded (waxing is too harsh around the eyes) by a professional, and then in the future, just tweeze any hairs that grow in.

Take a liner pencil or brush and hold it parallel along the side of your nose, straight up toward your forehead. Where the pencil and the brow meet is where the inner edge of your brow should begin. Any hairs between the two brows should be plucked.

Extend the pencil diagonally from your nostril toward the outside edge of your brow. Your eyebrow should end where the inside edge of the pencil hits the outside of the brow.

To find your arch, hold the pencil parallel to the outer edge of your iris. Where the pencil meets the brow is where the highest part, or arch, of your brow should be.

To pluck your brow, pull the skin taut at the outer edge of the brow and pluck in the direction of hair growth. Yes, you can and should tweeze unruly hairs above the brow. Get rid of that skinny, tapered tail too.

STEP 1:

you're hot

So, people think you're the summer intern? You have two choices—
turn 180 degrees in the other direction and find an entire new look, or embrace the
concept and be youthful, sophisticated, and head-turning.

she's got legs

While Keri was trying on lots of different
styles of jeans, I caught a glimpse of her legs and said,
"Whoa! Look at those gams! This girl should
be wearing skirts."

"Sex without a sense of humor is like French fries without the ketchup."

STEP 3:

mistaken identity

If people mistake Keri for a funny coed, I say let's go with it and make her a sexy funny coed by combining trendy layers with a classic car coat or a sequin miniskirt with a big Fair Isle sweater.

from a
different ankle

You'd think these wedges would go with this schoolgirly look,
but they're just too dumpy because they cut off Keri's legs at the ankles.
The sexy platform ankle boots continue the long black line of the skirt and the tights.
It's all about one long line from the foot on up.

STEP 4: show your assets

Keri, why on earth were you hiding your curves under loose-fitting tops and sweaters? Here's a dress that emphasizes Keri's waist, and that burgundy color is perfect for her. Shapely. '50s. Cocktail hour. Ladylike. A girl can do and say anything she wants when she looks like a lady.

How to look thinner

No surprise. This is the question I am asked most frequently. There are no hard-and-fast rules, but here's how to give the illusion that you just lost ten pounds:

- Wear black.
- Wear the right undergarments— a long-line bra or Spanx—for a leaner line.
- Dress in a monochromatic scheme— head-to-toe in one color or in a neutral tone.
- High heels—the higher the better.
- Jackets, dresses, and blouses with tailored shoulders. If you're narrow waisted, wear a belt to emphasize your tiniest part. If your waist is nowhere to be found, buy Empire dresses that are fitted just below the bust.
- The hem of a skirt should fall at the slimmest part of your leg, either below the calf or just above the knee.

"Remember this: No one is looking at your imperfections; they're all too busy worrying about their own."

Stunning!

FUNNY GIRL

Who says you can't look
youthful at any age?

• • •

Are You Inspired?

"The biggest thing I learned was not to be afraid to try something new, something different, something that
I wouldn't have pictured myself in. I have a big personality, but my clothes never matched it. I never dreamed of wearing a sequined skirt,
a big wooly sweater, cowboy boots, and a huge fur hat, but I can pull it off!
I love my easy makeup and my new eyebrow shape. My friends are always asking me for brow advice.
Can Mally come live with me?"

GROWN-UP SCHOOLGIRL

A great funny-sexy look—a sequined miniskirt
paired with a Fair Isle sweater. And if Keri can't wear this
crazy fur hat, then who can?

• • •

PARTY ON

A red sheath minidress with three-quarter-length
sleeves is a sophisticated but ageless style. Three bracelets
with hearts add a touch of whimsy.

• • •

Susan's inspiration board

animal prints • her cat and dog • figure skating • Barbra Streisand • Jacqueline Kennedy • The Beverly Hills Hotel •
Pink Tie Ball • purple figs • stilettos • Champagne prints

Question 22

"How do you think people see you style-wise?"

"Am I the queen of couture? No, but I think people would say I'm nicely dressed. When I was younger, I didn't have much need for evening clothes. Now that my life has gone from carpooling to charity events, my energies and priorities have changed, but my style hasn't."

Susan Shapiro, 56

Oh, yeah? Not the queen of couture? Well, why not? So much of inspiration and style is all about making your dreams come true.

You've said to yourself, "Ever since I was a little girl, I've wanted . . . a mink coat . . . diamond earrings . . . a one-of-a-kind couture dress designed for me."

Well, that time has come.

Barbra Streisand's "Don't Rain on My Parade" (played loud) is how Susan starts each day. Given her schedule, Susan has to be pumped. At the crack of dawn, she hits the ice at the local skating rink. Then it's off to work. And she is very active in the fight against breast cancer, volunteering for the Susan G. Komen Foundation North New Jersey Chapter, chairing a Pink Tie Ball, and writing the auction book for the event every year.

Susan was creating problems for herself that didn't really exist. She has an insanely great figure for a woman of 56, but she wasn't showing it off as well as she could and should. She has a great sense of style, alluring eyes, and a radiant face. But, like many women her age, Susan relies on tried-and-not-so-true tricks to make herself look younger. Shoulder-length blonde hair with highlights. Eye makeup applied the same way for years. Wearing only black at formal events. But they're all wrong for her.

They're so wrong (wrong makeup, undergarments, and hairstyle), they created problems that didn't have to be problems, because they all can be remedied.

Ladies, when an invitation reads "black tie requested," that refers to men and their tuxedos, not to you. Anyone can wear sophisticated black to a black-tie event, but that doesn't have to be you. Let everyone else wear black; think about an evening gown with a mix of glorious colors and various textures.

Susan is a beautiful woman who just needed a little TLC to become absolutely stunning.

FALSE EYELASHES TOP BARS? INDIVIDUALS?

BOB: TEASED IN BACK. SHOW AN EAR.

SHOW AS MUCH SKIN AS POSSIBLE

SASH.

* PINK LIP?
* RED LIP
NOT CLAY LIP !!!

SHIRT TOP FOR BLACK-TIE

Mermaid-ish shape

* TRY LONG LINE BODY-SHAPER

RIBS / WAIST / THIGHS.

Special occasions call for special effects. Wearing a fabulous gown to a black-tie event is the time to put on some false eyelashes for a lush look.

1 Curl your lashes with an eyelash curler.

2 Trim a full or half strip of eyelashes with scissors. Hold them up to your eyelash line to make certain the length is right.

3 Apply a very thin layer of glue to the top of the strip, adding an extra tiny dot of glue to the ends of the strip.

4 Wait 30 seconds for the glue to become tacky, and then apply the strip to the lash line, placing it just a bit in from the outer part of the eye. This opens up your eyes instead of drawing them down.

5 Marry your real lashes with the false lashes by applying eyeliner and a coat of mascara.

hair:
final cut

Cutting Susan's hair and parting it farther to the side immediately made her look more youthful, and it works for her active lifestyle.

STEP 1: sketches

"People often ask me, 'How do you design a dress for someone? What's your thought process?'"

"Never wait until you need an evening dress to buy one!"

Well, as soon as I meet someone, a lot of ideas start going through my head, and I don't hesitate to share them. I prefer to have our first meeting in a room full of clothes I designed so I can watch which pieces she gravitates toward. And it's a collaboration: The more information she shares about her likes and dislikes, the better. Once we have a starting point, where the dress is to be worn, her favorite color, her favorite body part that she wants to emphasize, etc., the rest falls into place. I like to challenge my clients and insist that they at least try on what I have in mind. Have some faith in the process and make a creative leap with me. Discover something new that looks great instead of relying on preconceived notions. More often than not, she's surprised and delighted, especially if it's a look she would never, ever have considered before.

making the muslin

"Muslin fitting" is fashion speak for an inexpensive dry run when designing a garment. (It refers to the fabric used as well as the actual stand-in item.) A muslin is where designers experiment with ideas, fit, and lines before cutting the costly fabrics for a final dress, suit, or other item. Much like a blueprint for a house, a muslin allows designers to make changes before actual construction begins. Are the sleeves the right length? Is the décolletage too deep or too high? Should the whole thing be shorter or longer?

Oh, and a muslin doesn't have to be made of muslin. Look at Susan's. While the top is muslin, the skirt uses inexpensive lace to show how the skirt and train of the gown will fall.

STEP 2: in the pink

Nothing beats owning a one-of-a-kind gown. Find an experienced seamstress who can work with you from concept to finished garment. (Use your inspiration board!) When having a gown made, you want richness and textures, so pay attention to every little detail, refining everything as you go along.

Susan's gown is an ultraluxe twist on the classic shirt-collar dress. The shirt bodice is made of iridescent pink silk taffeta with a sash that ties in the back. Embroidered chocolate brown French lace is layered over a skirt of pink and lilac circular-cut chiffon ruffles finished with a picot edging.

The dress was almost finished, but something about it wasn't quite right to my eye. That pink shirt just wasn't flattering enough for such an elegant gown. It was replaced with deep, dark chocolate brown for over-the-top perfection.

STEP 3:

the glitter

An evening gown such as this one calls for some of the
finest of fine jewelry, but not too much. No necklace. No earrings.
One arm: Four bracelets, two rings. From the top: Micropavé-set pink
diamonds in rose gold; diamond bangle; table diamonds in an
art deco setting; and a chunky bracelet of sapphires, topazes, quartzes,
and crystals. The pinky ring is a pink diamond set among white diamonds.
The other ring is diamonds and rubies set in yellow gold.
If you don't own the right jewelry, then borrow or rent some.
And there's plenty of you-could-fool-me
costume jewelry out there.

*"Don't limit
custom-made clothes
to fancy-occasion dresses. If you
have a favorite pair of
pants or a skirt that you adore
and fit you just so, have
a seamstress copy it
for you."*

Are You Inspired?

"When Isaac suggested I cut my hair, I decided to go for it! I instantly fell in love with my haircut and my new look.
It's difficult to explain, but I have a new attitude. Maybe because the look is younger. I liked my look before, but now I love it and so
does my husband, Terry. He claims he has a new wife. After thirty-five years, that's a good thing!
Isaac made me feel like a fairy-tale princess. And my skating coach said I'm skating better. When I laughed at that,
he said it was no different from putting on an outfit that you feel great in. When you feel good about yourself, it shows in everything
you do. Speaking of great outfits, . . . the gown that Isaac created for me is stunning. I can't believe it's mine! I know this
sounds corny, but I look at it every day. I can't wait to wear it and get that
fairy-tale princess feeling again!"

Divine!

since we're on the topic of evening wear

That can be a scary term. Relax, ladies, it's easier than you think. I say have fun with it. The key to looking great in the evening is to look original. Try to look different from others without looking out of place. When everyone else is wearing black, stand out in a bold, bright color. When everyone else is wearing a dress that falls to the floor, shock them with a short gold brocade suit. But try not to overdo it. Focus on one thing: Will it be a statement necklace, a stunning pair of earrings, or really big hair? You decide. I encourage you to stop saying, "I just want to look *not so bad*" and instead say, "I want to look fabulous."

"Don't wait for an invitation to buy an evening dress.
When you see something you love, buy it!"

Regan's inspiration board

Goodfellas • *A Bar at the Folies-Bergére* by Edouard Manet • stand of trees • Boston College Arts Festival • Sydney, Australia •
seashells • Audrey Hepburn • cathedrals • *Another Wonderful Day* by Dick LaBonte

Question 11

"What's your biggest style challenge?"

"I just graduated from college and I have worn some kind of uniform all of my life. From kindergarten through high school, I was stuck in a drab parochial school outfit. My uniform for four years at Boston College was a hoodie and sweatpants in the school colors of maroon and gold. I want to learn how to dress like a woman."

Regan Murphy, 22

All through elementary and high school and college, Regan wore a uniform of sorts. Her parochial school uniforms and hoodie-and-sweats in her college colors left her no opportunity to show off her artistic side. Now that she was entering the so-called real world, Regan wasn't sure how she should dress.

There's nothing wrong with having a uniform or a style that you wear every day. After all, I wear my own version of a uniform every day. Who doesn't? But what you want is your own personal uniform that makes you stand out.

Since Regan's first job is in the New York art world, it's time to create a new uniform—one that shows off a sense of grown-up style, which she has but has been hiding. Regan's wardrobe colors of choice were a yawn.

Brown—lots and lots and lots of brown—along with blah teal blue, drab greens, and murky reds. Even her lipstick was brownish. The artwork and photos on Regan's inspiration board didn't really say too much about where to go visually. They did give me a sense of who Regan is: A smart sober girl who should have a dignified wardrobe.

I wanted to see Regan wear gray, navy, and black with an occasional splash of red and oatmeal as accents. I told her that she has to carefully consider each and every item she purchases. I want her to have fun when she shops yet remember that she's entering womanhood. Her clothes have to be more meaningful and versatile. She's at a turning point in life. It's time for her cast off childhood and have fun as an adult.

LAYER HAIR.

"FINISH" EYEBROWS.

* SKIN CARE IS NEEDED: DERMO.? FACIALIST?

* MAKEUP EMPHASIZE EYES.

ACCENTUATE HER WAIST.

PEEP-TOE

BOOT: SUEDE?

LOW-CUT FLAT. (MAYBE A COLOR)

makeup: shape up

Give those brows some shape to make Regan's eyes pop.
Reapply mascara throughout the day to give
your eyes a boost. Be sure to wipe off any smudges
underneath your eyes, or you'll look tired.
Lips dry and flaky? Gently exfoliate your lips with
a baby toothbrush before applying liner and lipstick.
Your skin is the first thing people notice,
so it should always be radiant and blemish-free—
especially once you're an adult. I noticed that
Regan's skin needed help; read about her amazing
transformation on the following page. Good skin care
is a matter of finding the right program
for your individual skin type—
and sticking to it.

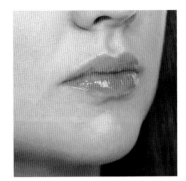

"If you really want style, you have to work at it. It's not easy."

hair: let it down

What was with the bun? It's too
matronly for young Regan.
She can and should wear her hair
long. The secret to great-looking
long hair? Get it trimmed,
shaped, and, if necessary,
thinned out regularly.

Renowned aesthetician Alla Katkov of Miano Viél Salon and Spa in New York has seen—and solved—every skin problem imaginable. So when Regan mentioned her ongoing struggle with acne—even taking a course of antibiotics that worked only temporarily—Alla stepped up to the challenge.

At Regan's first visit, Alla reviewed her current skin care regimen. Regan was using a much-advertised three-step program that was drying out her skin but not getting rid of the acne or getting to the underlying problem. Using drying cleansers and scrubs, then applying moisturizers to combat dry skin results in a vicious circle; you use more cleanser to get rid of the surface oil from the moisturizer, then apply more moisturizer because the skin is so dry.

At the first session, Alla's goal was to bring Regan's skin to its proper pH level to make her skin less appealing to the bacteria that cause acne. Alla used fragrance-free cleansing milk and then applied a toner and a pH-normalizing complex to balance her skin's pH. Warm steam was aimed at Regan's face as a nonabrasive oatmeal scrub was applied. With the steam still going, Alla used an electric rotating brush to exfoliate. Clean facial sponges dipped in cool—not hot or cold—water removed the scrub. Alla carefully performed extractions. Gentle electric impulses zap bacteria, tighten pores, and diffuse redness from the skin's surface. An alpha hydroxy peel follows to get rid of Regan's scarring, and then a Purifying Therma Mud Mask to remove impurities, slough off dead cells, and tighten pores. Alla finished with a soothing application of the pH-normalizing complex. Regan left with new Terme di Saturnia products, Alla's favorite, and instructions for a twice-daily regime of cleansing, rinsing, toning, and normalizing.

After just three sessions—each one different—with Alla, Regan's skin was glowing on the day of her photo shoot! No more inflammations. Her skin was soft, pliable, and lively, not dry. Scarring and brown spots were gone. All due to Alla's magic fingers and the right products.

Basic skin care advice, and what to look for in a facialist:

- Alla knows that sun worshippers like Regan won't give up sunbathing no matter how dire the warnings, so she recommends the following: Wear a hat with a big brim—not a baseball cap or sun visor. Use sunblock, not sunscreen, with UVA/UVB protection, an SPF of 35 to 45, and titanium oxide. Reapply it regularly. Wash your skin as soon as possible after sunning with a cleansing foam and an aqua sponge, and apply toner to keep pores from becoming clogged with oily sunblock.

- Even with the best skin care regimen, monthly breakouts can't always be avoided, because they are hormonal. Continue with your routine and apply Desert Spring Deep Action Drying Lotion, a favorite of Alla's, on spots.

- Waxing facial hair can cause burns and sometimes scarring, especially on sensitive skin. Alla prefers that her clients have facial hair either temporarily removed by threading or eliminated permanently by electrolysis or laser. While permanent hair removal is more expensive up front, it's cheaper in the long run. After a few sessions on a particular area, you will never have to deal with the cost or pain of waxing or threading again.

- Use only fragrance-free and alcohol-free products. Alcohol dries the skin, and products with fragrances often contain alcohol.

- A facial should be customized to individual skin type and age. These determine the specific treatment and products used.

- A facial should include the areas above the breasts—the upper chest, neck, and tops of shoulders—as well as the face.

- A top-notch facial should last 90 minutes.

- Remember the four steps for morning and night: Cleanse, rinse, tone, and normalize.

- At night, apply a vitamin night cream to the eye area.

- Improper extractions cause pitting and scarring. Only a qualified skin care specialist knows how to do them; don't try them yourself.

- Once you find a facialist who understands and knows your skin, it's important to have a facial on a monthly basis.

- Here's my favorite tip from Alla: Always walk out of a facial looking better, not worse or red or blotchy, than when you walked in. Your skin should be plump and glowing.

STEP 1: when and how to splurge

Knowing when to splurge is an art. There are just two rules: Splurge on the most classic item in the world. You will have and cherish it forever. Splurge on the most insane thing in the world. You will have and cherish it forever.

Still not sure about being indulgent? If you sleep on it for a bit, how do you know that that handbag or those dangly earrings will still be there? Ask the salesperson how many are in stock and if the store can reorder if they sell out; then decide how long you have before making up your mind.

STEP 2: buy the basics

Hey, listen, you young ladies just starting out: You'll need more than just that diploma to land your dream job. Invest in some starter wardrobe pieces for interviews, as well as for going to work once you get that job and heading out after hours with your new colleagues. A great tailored all-seasons suit in a neutral color. (Jacket, trousers, and skirt.) Black trousers. White T-shirts. Button-down shirts. Some trousers and skirts. A few blouses. A shearling coat or a lighter trench. A good classic handbag made to be worn and worn and worn. ("Oh, this bag? I've been carrying it for years!")

"WHEN YOU GET DRESSED, WHO ARE YOU DRESSING FOR, REGAN?"

"I dress for myself, but if I am going to see a particular group of people I want to impress, I'll sometimes make an effort."

"Sometimes? No, Regan, when getting dressed, think about the community you live in. Ask yourself who you are and what/who you are dressing for. How should you look in a particular situation? What will it take that day to make yourself look and feel great?"

If you're like Mary Kate (page 91), Janine (page 43), or millions of other women of all sizes and shapes, buying off-the-rack clothes can be frustrating. Ill-fitting clothes give you a sloppy, I-don't-care look. How much better a woman looks in a well-tailored jacket that lies flat across the back, doesn't tug at the armpits, and falls to the right sleeve length. Whether you're a plus size, a petite, or anything in between, a good tailor or seamstress ensures that you can be as stylish as everyone else.

Here are some suggestions from seamstresses Shannon O'Hara and Claudia de Sousa, who hemmed skirts, shortened sleeves, took in and let out some of the clothes shown in this book.

- If a garment fits the shoulders, bust, and hips properly, then anything else—sleeve length, hem, waist, back—can be adjusted with tailoring.
- Have the tailor pin everything. Don't be afraid to speak up, saying that the hem is too long or the sleeves aren't short enough.
- Since every garment can vary slightly, even if it is the same style and size from the same manufacturer, take the time to try on each piece and have it pinned. Asking a seamstress to match one pair of pants to another, for instance, is a waste of money, since each pair may have a slightly different rise, which affects the inseam.
- It's much easier to make a too-big piece smaller than to make a too-small item bigger, because

there's no seam allowance and the original stitching lines may be noticeable.
- To find a local tailor, look at your neighborhood websites. Take advantage of department store tailors and seamstresses; they are familiar with the retailer's clothing lines.
- When being fitted, wear the shoes you plan to wear with that outfit. If you always pair two-inch high-heeled boots with jeans, wear them when having your pants hemmed.

- When jeans are the right length, your legs will look longer. To achieve this, make sure there's a small fabric break over the top of your shoes. If you can pinch ¾ inch or a full inch on the top of your shoe, then the break is perfect.
- How to judge good tailoring? The finishing—the stitching on the hem of jeans, the thread color, the vent in the back of a jacket—should look just like the original item.

STEP 3: update the classics

To build on your basic wardrobe, start adding classic items that are more interesting but timeless. Wide-legged trousers. Think about prints as well as solid colors. Blouses with small, understated prints provide a little individuality yet are still sophisticated. Change up the trousers look with a red cashmere cardigan and T-strap shoes. Add a black-and-white cocktail dress with an elegant evening coat to your wardrobe. A knee-length short-sleeved dress never goes out of style.

Quality versus quantity

. . . .

If you learn nothing else from this book, take away this one all-important lesson: Teach yourself to buy less stuff. Spend more money on a few exceptional, high-quality items that you will wear again and again—cashmere sweaters, a classic trench coat, a timeless dress.

Save up for those half-carat $900 diamond-and-platinum studs. Or put your daily $4 for cappuccino in an envelope marked "Coach bag." (Do the math: $4 multiplied by 5 days multiplied by 4 weeks equals $80—times 5 months equals $400!) Quality wins over quantity every time.

STEP 4: the unexpected

Classic doesn't mean boring or safe; it can be cool and unique like this shorts suit.
There's no reason for Regan to get lost in the world of "business clothes."
Don't worry, she'll still be able to pay off those college loans and have
enough money left to buy classics, especially if she looks for the unexpected in unexpected
places. Regan's shorts suit comes from uniqlo, and her traditional car coat with
an animal print lining is from Target®.

I ask
you!

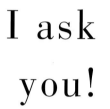

Are You Inspired?

"When I get dressed in the morning, I'm a whole lot more creative. I've always thought of myself as a creative person, but not when it came to my clothes. Now I feel like a part of my personality is coming through with what I wear, and that is very exciting. I bought some good-quality blazers to go with really colorful blouses. Layering prints and wearing bold colors is something I never even considered. Now it's my look; I own it. I bought a bunch of inexpensive colored and textured tights and pair them with skirts and boots (or flats) for work. I'm a walking ad for my own style."

THE FINAL TOUCH

A simple pendant on a gold chain is young yet classic.
It hits in the right place in her décolletage.

• • •

CHANGE UP

Regan can evolve her wardrobe throughout
the week by wearing the dress with the coat, the
suit jacket, or the sweater.

• • •

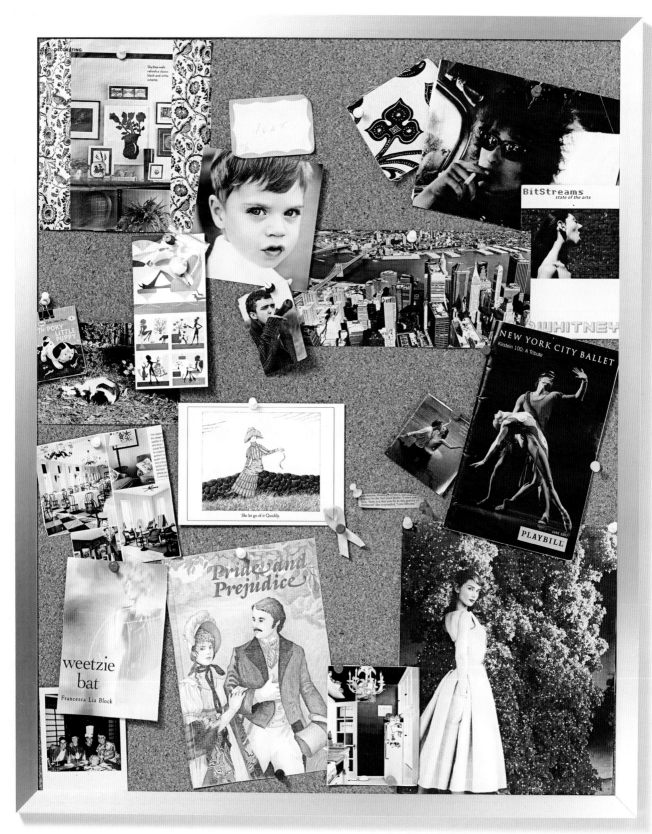

Rebecca's inspiration board

Pride and Prejudice • Bob Dylan • Manhattan • black-and-white decor • *Weetzie Bat* • Edward Gorey •
Audrey Hepburn • lilacs • *The Poky Little Puppy* • New York City Ballet

Question 8

"**What's the one item
in your closet that
you wear again and
again and again?**"

"*Jeans. When going
on a date or out
with friends, I always
fall back on jeans.
I want out of my
denim trap. I want
to be chic, no jeans
or a 'going-out shirt'
in sight!*"

Rebecca Frazer, 31

Listen up, girls of America, if I see one more of you heading out for a night on the town with your gal pals in a pair of jeans, your "going-out top," and your fancy heels, I'm going to scream.

I get why you do it. I get that it's easy.

You think the jeans are casual and say I-don't-care-all-that-much in a safe way. The top is cute and sexy and just different enough from the ones all the other girls are wearing. The heels are sexy. And they cost you a month's salary.

Do you get why that look is boring? It does nothing to tell us who you are. You may feel sexy and safe, but that won't get you noticed.

If there's a poster girl for this look, it's Rebecca. Jeans for friends. Jeans for work. Jeans on a date. Jeans, jeans, jeans, jeans, jeans. They were the centerpiece of Rebecca's wardrobe. A denim dead-end. Especially since she has an absolutely exquisite figure—tall, thin, and long-legged—and a smile that is a window into who she really is.

What would be left in her closet if all her jeans were taken away? A couple of A-line skirts and a few undistinguished dresses. While a great pair of jeans is a necessity in every woman's wardrobe, jeans were Rebecca's security blanket. And a dull one at that.

Rebecca's dependence on jeans came out of not really knowing herself or her sense of style. Some questions needed asking and answering. What's appropriate in your world? How can you express yourself with your style? Who are you going to be seen by? How does the world perceive you? Rebecca works in publishing, and her goal is to move up the editorial/corporate ladder—but women executives simply don't wear jeans to the office. It sends the wrong signal. So it's time for a more sophisticated work look. About her social life, Rebecca says, "I want my style to evolve. I want to look cute but also my age . . . and smart, and fun, and down-to-earth—and to stand out from the crowd."

So what inspires Rebecca? Her favorite fictional character is Elizabeth Bennett, the spunky, independent, irreverent heroine in Jane Austen's *Pride and Prejudice*, often played by spunky, independent, and stylish actresses. New York City feeds her soul—the people, the architecture, the energy. So where's that sophisticated, edgy New York look?

Oh, Rebecca, time to wake up from your jeans coma!

FIX "BROKEN" EYEBROWS.

BANGS?!*

SKIRTS!!!

* GO AS BARE AS POSSIBLE
GORGEOUS SHOULDERS
GORGEOUS HANDS
GORGEOUS LEGS
GORGEOUS

SLIM SKIRT

MINI SKIRT

PARTY SKIRT

hair: bangs or no bangs?

A good trick is to hold your hair above your eyebrows to see how you will look with bangs. Definitely bangs for Rebecca.

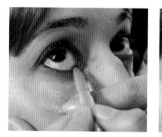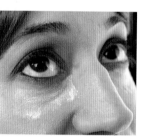

makeup: less is so much more

Rebecca took the thin eyebrows too far, so Mally filled hers in with a brunet pencil to make them fuller and longer. It's all about an unfussy, smoky look here, not the color. Rebecca's upper and lower lids are lined with black eyeliner and then smudged with a cotton swab or the tip of a finger. Apply that eyeliner as close to the lash line as possible, so there's no white space between the lash line and eyelashes. Open your eyes even more by applying a bit of concealer to the inside bridge of your nose.

STEP 1: put on a dress

Wearing a dress is just as easy as putting on a pair of jeans. Slip it over your head, and that's it. Talk about an instant outfit. And never before have there been so many great dresses for all women. Show those legs!

"If you want others to treat you like a supermodel, it has to start somewhere. It has to start with your perception of yourself. Supermodel is as supermodel does."

tights and hose

My number one choice is a bare leg. It's sexy and young looking. But hose are such a personal subject, and some women just don't feel dressed without them. Every woman has her idea of what is proper and what isn't.

On the other hand, tights and hose can be wonderfully slimming. Layer one pair of hose on top of another, like sheer hose under textured or fishnet over opaque.

I adore opaque tights. There is no limit to who can wear them. Young women look polished. Middle-aged women appear instantly younger. I've even seen women in their seventies wearing tiny, short skirts with opaque hose, and they look incredible. As we get older, it's harder to look dressed up. So embrace it and dress down a little. Keep it casual, shorten the skirt a tad, and wear surprising hose.

Two things I do hate: Sheer colored hose, like sheer red, and nude hose—they have sneaky, undercover names like taupe, beige, bare, ecru. Stay away from both; they are ugly.

STEP 2:
wear black and white

I usually encourage women to wear color, but here black and white are the first steps. Start with black tights, and she's halfway there. A tweed or solid black skirt? A black or striped tank top? A jacket or a sweater? Animal-print flats, ankle boots, or heels? Every one of these looks is just great.

STEP 3:
when in doubt, wear black

Don't know what else to wear besides jeans when planning to go out? Try all black. But to stand out, again, you must mix patterns and textures.

A perfect example of how a look looks special with four different textures, all in black: Start with a lacy bra or a camisole, then add a lacy skirt. Top with a sparkling tweedy sweater. Make the whole thing less serious with black patent high heels with a bow.

This look will get you noticed.

Are You Inspired?

"It's great to be wearing skirts and dresses every day instead of just jeans. And I am having a love affair with opaque-black, semi-opaque, and colorful tights. For the first time in a very long time, I feel like there is something fresh and fun in everything I am wearing. I am standing out from the crowd, which can be tough in New York City. I love that my clothes are now saying something besides, 'Look at my cute jeans.' I have a whole new mission every morning when I get dressed.

"Just by cutting bangs, my hair is styled. I can pull it back in a jiffy and have a new look, not just a sloppy, boring ponytail. My bangs give me a little something extra to make my look more put together. I'm told that one of the signs of growing up is having a hairstyle—I'm getting there!"

SHORT AND SWEET

Sexy but fun. How? By wearing all black,
but in four different textures.

• • •

HOLLY GOLIGHTLY

Accessories—red tights and heels,
black handbag, and three-quarter-length gloves—
totally change the look of the dress.

• • •

Wow!

MAKE AN ENTRANCE

Sometimes you
just need to wear sparkles.
All sparkles.

• • •

WHAT YOU NEED

Think of your closet as a living, breathing being. It changes from day to day, month to month, and season to season. In many ways, you can think of it in the same way you think of your kitchen pantry. You stock your pantry with basics: Pasta. Flour. Canned goods. Grains. Reliable staples that can be used with other favorite ingredients.

You want to stock your closet the same way, but with clothing staples: items that can be used in lots of different ways.

The following pages highlight the most basic categories—shoes, bags, jewelry, and bras—items that all women need in their wardrobes.

WHAT YOU NEED: SHOES

Shoes makes a woman sexy: How sexy is your choice, whether you want to play it down one day in mannish oxfords or up the next with fetish high heels. Can you ever have enough shoes? It's your call.

RAIN BOOTS
These rubber riding boots are a little chicer than your average pair of galoshes.

COWBOY BOOTS
The perfect way to bring any look down to earth.

BLACK BOOTS
Do I need to tell you why you should have black boots?

ANKLE STRAP SANDALS
For night, they're a standard; for day, they're a surprise.

T-STRAP HEELS
For day, they're a standard; for night, they're a surprise.

BLACK PUMPS
The definition of basic.

JEWELED EVENING SANDALS
Everyone needs a bit of extravagance.

ANIMAL PRINT SHOES
Leopard print is the soul of wit.

EVENING SHOES
If you want a little more sex appeal for just that moment.

BELGIAN LOAFERS

If they were good enough for Garbo,
they're good enough for you.

BALLET FLATS

Take the time to find the right ones.

WEDGE SANDALS

For dressy, these are casual. For
casual, they are a surprise.

COTTON MARY JANES

A lot of style for almost no money.

DRIVING SHOE
Even your most utilitarian shoes
can be candy coated.

FLIP FLOPS
You'd be surprised how much style
these bring to the party.

SNEAKERS
I love classic sneakers as a fashion staple.
Save your running shoes for running.

METALLIC FLIP FLOPS
These inexpensive sandals nicely
show off an expensive pedicure.

WHAT YOU NEED: BAGS

Your handbag is the most emotional purchase you make. It has to be just right—fashionable as well as functional. You hold it close, and it stays with you at all times ("Where's my bag?"). Your handbag is an impression maker. These are the handbag categories you need; the individual choices for each one are personal.

SUMMER BAG
Choose this one with good humor, and dispose of it after one season.

EVENING CLUTCH
The more you spend, the longer you'll have it.

EVERYDAY TOTE BAG
Other factors besides appearance are at work here: Is it useful? Is it lightweight? Is it versatile? Ask yourself those questions.

EVERYDAY SHOULDER BAG
In a world full of shoulder bags, have one that's really simple.

POCKETBOOK
For lunch or cocktails, this will get
you through.

COMPUTER TOTE
I like one that doesn't look like
a computer tote.

ASPIRATIONAL HANDBAG
Every girl needs a dream. Go for it.

ECO-BAG
Never go shopping without one.
Out: paper and plastic. In: reusable.

WEEKEND BAG
Size matters. Keep it medium-sized
so you won't overpack.

WHAT YOU NEED: JEWELRY

I prefer to see women wear big bold pieces one at a time as a focus rather than piling on a lot of jewelry, but everyone has her own jewelry needs. Some like a lot, some like a little. To start, you have to discover which type you are. However, these are the essential pieces that every woman should have.

PEARLS ON WIRES
Sexy and proprietary.

DIAMOND STUDS
Elegant.

CHANDELIER EARRINGS
Make your neck look longer.

PLAIN GOLD HOOPS
A girl's best friend.

COCKTAIL RINGS
Break the ice.

BAND RING
Make a commitment.

CHARM BRACELET
Not only gorgeous, but a great keepsake.

SPLURGE BANGLE BRACELETS
Add instant chic.

INEXPENSIVE BANGLE BRACELETS
Make the plainest outfit exotic.

STATEMENT CUFF OR BRACELET
Instant glamour

PEARLS
Always appropriate.

STATEMENT NECKLACE
Express yourself!

CHARMS ON GOLD CHAINS
More than beautiful, these should
be meaningful.

WHAT YOU NEED: WATCHES

Wearing a watch isn't just about telling time, or we'd all be wearing ten dollar watches from the flea market. A watch makes a style statement about who you are—just like everything else you wear. And that means you need a few different ones to complete your many looks. Watches range in price from almost nothing to piles of money, from plastic to vintage gold.

CARTIER TANK WATCH
Because it's for every day. It will never go out of style.

FUN WATCH
There are so many inexpensive watches out there, there's no reason to be late.

LARGE DIVER'S WATCH
For dressy, this is a surprise; for everyday, it's indispensable.

MAN'S WATCH
Always good to bend a gender. When you're wearing the most feminine dress or suit, a mannish watch is a must.

BRACELET WATCH
Here's one way to feminize a watch. It's not essential, but if you're going to have a bracelet watch make sure it's as wonderful as this one.

ROLEX WATCH
If you aspire to a name brand, go for it.

DIAMOND EVENING WATCH
Because every woman has one already and/or can get her hands on one when a relative dies. If not, she should kill a relative.

WHAT YOU NEED: BRAS

Question 13: "When was the last time you were fitted for a bra?"
"Uh…never." (Janine)

Half the women in this book were wearing the wrong size or style bra, which is common to 8 out of 10 American women, before Gail Oliver, Regional Consultant Manager at Wacoal-America, stepped in to help out.

Girls, get those girls some help!

According to Gail, American women prefer a smooth, round, no-seam look, while their European sisters like bras with lace and frills and a projected, breast forward style. What's that all about?

Most women wear a band that's too big and a cup size that's too small. For some reason, American women like to think they are a size 36C or 38C—that's a small cup size—when the average sizes are 34D or 34DD. If you think you need a larger size, first go up in a cup size, not the band, until the fit is right.

Visit a fit specialist at any department or lingerie store for a complimentary consultation after a weight gain or loss of seven to ten pounds, or after a pregnancy and once nursing is over. Go for a refitting once a year no matter what. Even if there's no weight gain or loss, gravity and time take their toll, and bras that once fit well just don't anymore.

The fitter will first measure your band size under the breasts. If the measurement is an even number of 34 inches or less, she will add 4 inches; if the measurement is an odd number of 34 inches or less, she will add 5 inches to get your band size. Measurements between 35 and 38 inches add 2 inches if the number is even, 3 inches if the number is odd. Between 39 or more, no inches are added if the measurement is an even number; just one inch is added for an odd number. An example: Two inches are added to a band measurement of 36 inches resulting in a band size of 38.

To determine cup size, the fitter measures around the fullest part of the bust. The difference between the band measurement and the bust measurement determines the cup size. Every inch over the band size refers to a cup size. One inch is an A, two a B, 3 a C, 4 a D and so on.

Once you have the bra on, it should lift, separate, and contain. To make sure the bra is right for you, here are a couple of hints from Gail:

• The middle section of the bra between the cups is called tacking; that should hit right at the breast bone.

• Stand with one arm bent at a 90 degree right angle. Your breast should be close to equal distance between the elbow and shoulder.

• When you raise your arms above your head, your breasts should not come out below the band. If it does, the band is probably too big and the cup too small.

• Walk, move, sit—is it comfortable? Does it cut or feel tight anywhere? Take off the shoulder straps. If the bra fits properly, it will stay in place.

• When purchasing a new bra you should be fitted to close the middle hook. That way you can adjust it looser or tighter.

• Always have the straps adjusted correctly for proper alignment. Readjust after washing and wearing to keep the proper alignment.

• Wash a new bra before wearing. Place the cups inside one another, hook the bra together, and place in a mesh laundry bag. Wash in mild detergent—no bleach—and cold water. Hang or lie flat to dry. Wash your bras after every wearing, and each one should last 100 washings.

As long as the subject is breasts, remember to perform a monthly breast self-exam. For detailed information how to do a BSE, go to Susan G. Komen for the Cure (www.komen.org).

KILLER SEXY BRA

"Not comfortable, but so hot looking,
it won't be on for very long."
JENNY LURIE

"Oh, it closes in the front?
Great fit and gorgeous detailing."
MEGHAN HORSTMANN

SPORTS BRA

"Wish I could wear this all the time."
ERIKA STAIR

"So supportive, so comfortable.
No flopping around when I ran."
AMANDA SINCLAIR

Do you wear the same shirt or pants every day? Of course not. Same goes for bras. And different clothes require specific bras. Wear beige or ecru bras under white shirts for business attire; white shows through, flesh tones don't. When going out, make your bra part of your outfit; wear a contrasting—a black bra under a pink shirt—color that shows through or peeks out.

Now that you know your correct bra size, which styles will look and fit best? Like everything else, you have to try on lots of bras to find the right ones for you. They are a matter of fit and preference, taste, and needs. Be realistic about what kind of bra is realistic for you and what strikes your fancy. While bras are wardrobe workhorses, providing a true foundation for everything that goes on top, they can and should be fun. You'll feel stylish knowing you're wearing a hot number, even if no one else does.

Now, since it didn't make sense for me to try the bras on, some of the women in my studio volunteered. Little did they know that they would have to try on dozens of them. These brave women tried out bras for the weekend and then reported back on Monday. Why? Bras, like shoes, often feel just fine in the store, but some dig and cut after wearing them for a couple of hours.

Responses ranged from "One flattened me so much that I looked like I was in *Shakespeare in Love*." to a group high five for the great fit and comfort of the Champion sports bra. Small-breasted women liked one strapless while the same bra cut into the upper chest of girls with larger girls, who preferred another style. Cheap bras—those $10.99 specials from trendy international chain stores looked and felt—uh—cheap. Here are some more opinions:

STRAPLESS BRA
"Wow, a strapless bra that's comfortable and
actually stays up on my small boobs." JL
"Way too much elastic. This one left marks
across the top." AS

UNDERWEAR AS OUTWEAR
"Great fit, and boy, what a statement it makes under
a sheer blouse." ES
"So comfy, yet so Austin Powers!" JL

LACY REVEALING NUMBER
"Might as well be wearing nothing." AS
"No support and itchy lace, but who cares when
wearing with a v-neck top?" MH

CONTOUR MOLDED BRA FOR SMALLER BREASTS
"This is my new favorite for fit, but I'd cut off the ribbon." MH
"Made me look bigger and very enhancing." JL

SEAMLESS BRA

"This Spanx Bra-llelujah! held 'em in and felt
  like I was wearing nothing." JL

"Really supportive and my boob shape was
  perfect in a t-shirt." ES

PEEK-A-BOO BRA

"I'd never spend the big bucks on this Little Mermaid-like
  bra with gems …but it was fun to try on. I'm such a
  sucker for this stuff." JL

SEAMED LACE UNDERWIRE

"Who needs a underwire bra to make
  me bigger? I'm big enough!" AS

"Loved that underwire! It made me look bigger!" JL

"Great style…if you're an old maid." MH

RACERBACK

"That racerback made my boobs look funny and flattened me!" AS

"Too much fabric on the cup that wasn't smooth." ES

WHAT YOU NEED: INSTANT STYLE IDEAS

Let's say it's Tuesday, and you just can't seem to pull yourself together. You need an instant style boost. Here are a few ideas...

SUNGLASSES
If you must hide, hide behind dark sunglasses.

WHITE SHIRT
The simplest way to purify your day is with a white shirt.

COCKTAIL RING
Make a point with your pointer: Try an oversized cocktail ring.

RED LIPSTICK
Nothing makes anyone smile like a smile. And nothing is "smilier" than a bright red smile.

BRIGHT COLORED SWEATERS
Bold cashmere sweaters bring life to and complement any drab color you're wearing.

BLACK EYELINER
Overcome boredom with dark eyeliner.

TRENCH COAT
One always adds mystery.

CHANDELIER EARRINGS
Nothing focuses a look like dangling earrings.

BLACK TIGHTS
The morning after? Black tights hide
a multitude of sins.

BLACK PATENT PUMPS
Every girl needs snappy black patent shoes.
If they don't pep up you and your wardrobe,
nothing will.

BANDANAS
They're a major source of color vitamins.
Wear at least two every day.

THE STYLE WORKBOOK

There's only one way to be excellent at something. You have to practice. Having style is no different. It's like going to the gym or getting in the kitchen and cooking. The more you do it, the stronger and the better you become. The following style exercises are designed to make you use your eyes and your intuition and to help you get on the road to great personal style. Start flexing that style muscle now.

mirrors!
lights! action!

I can't stress enough the importance of having the right mirrors and lighting. Lighting is everything. Start being sensitive to it. When looking in a mirror, notice when the lighting is right and flatters you. Try to recreate that lighting as much as possible in your everyday world. It sounds ridiculous, but it's easier to plan ahead a little than to suffer the consequences of bad lighting. All actors and actresses understand this principal, and it's largely because of lighting that they look great all the time. You must have a full-length mirror; a three-way mirror would be heaven if you have the room. Your makeup mirror should be mounted in a well-lit location. Of course, a Hollywood-style dressing-room mirror with small lightbulbs around all the sides would be fabulous. But I'm realistic, and a couple of well-placed desk lamps will do the trick. Light should never shine from below or above. The light should be aimed directly at your face and, ideally, reflect off the wall. I always note the restaurants and hotels where the lighting is flattering . . . and go back quite often!

TAKE STOCK

Clothing stores close to take inventory several times a year. You should do the same by rotating your stock—and not just seasonally. You will never have style if the same three or four shirts are always front and center in your closet.

If your closet looks messy, it's time to take inventory. Pull everything out and pile it on the bed. Make an honest assessment of what you wear and what you don't. If the last time you wore that plaid skirt was more than a year ago, it's probably time to say good-bye or to figure out a fresh way to wear it. That printed silk shirt you used to wear all the time now seems tired. But what if you pair it with something more casual such as jeans or mix it with animal-pattern trousers? Clothing doesn't always go out of style; it sometimes just needs a boost or some rethinking.

Don't overlook your shoes and boots. Take your sandals to the shoemaker at the end of summer, your boots at the end of winter. When their wearing season rolls around again, you won't groan about their condition. Instead, it will seem as if you bought a bunch of new shoes.

A messy closet is depressing. Be nice to your clothes. Don't shove or cram things into your closet. How will you ever know what you have if you can't see or find anything? Hang your clothes on wooden hangers. Fold sweaters properly before putting them in drawers. Then it will be much easier to pull together looks every day. No more staring at the your closet in the morning, hoping that an outfit will magically jump out at you.

If you really have a problem organizing yourself, hire a professional. It will be money well spent.

Practice your makeup

I hear again and again "I love the look of liquid eyeliner, but it's too hard to do myself." You'd be surprised how easy it can be if you practice. Trying out new make-up looks is just as important as trying on clothes and accessories. Practice makeup techniques—creating smoky eyes, applying fake eyelashes, mixing colors, applying eyeliner, contouring your cheekbones—to perfection. And remember: blend, blend, blend!

TRY EVERYTHING ON

I know we are all short on time when getting ready, but you need to make time to try things on. Even I have to sweat a bit to achieve a perfectly styled outfit (I take a picture to remember the outfit for my inspiration board!). Don't wait until the last minute. Think about what you want to wear in advance and then try on as many variations as you can. Look in the mirror from every angle. Is it too tight, too short, or uncomfortable? Taking time to find the right mix will allow you to feel so much more confident when you walk out the door.

GO SHOPPING. DON'T BUY A THING

What do I mean? "Just Looking" (page 23) is what I mean! Now that you have gone through your closet and drawers, you have a good sense of what you need. Rather than being impulsive and buying everything, though, first visit lots of stores and try on all kinds of clothing, shoes, and accessories. You will learn more about yourself and your likes and dislikes than you could ever imagine. If you realize that all you have in your closet are jeans and tops, try on tons of dresses and skirts. If you have only flats and "sensible shoes," try on every pair of heels you can find. If there is anything you feel you cannot live without, put it on hold. Go home. If when you wake up the next morning it's the first thing that pops into your head, buy it.

TRY THEM ON—AGAIN

Try on your new purchases as soon as you get home. It's sometimes hard to make the right call in a tiny dressing room with poor lighting. Do your new things look better at home? If not, you'll know. Take them back right away.

Err on the Side of Confidence

Too often women dress in a way that hides their best features. Try this: Get naked in front of a mirror. What do you love about your body? If it's your legs, wear the highest heels you can for a week. If it's your tiny waist, accentuate it with a belt every day. If you've got it, show it.

Back to the Future

Go deep into your closet and find those red jeans or that neon blouse from years ago that you just can't part with. Try the red jeans with a navy-and-white boatneck sailor shirt or pair the neon blouse with a black skirt. Give those sentimental items a reason to take up valuable closet real estate by putting together new looks with them. I challenge you to make use out of everything in your closet. Soon what you once thought of as cast-offs will become favorite pieces.

WORTH EVERY PENNY

Making a big-ticket purchase like an evening gown or a winter coat requires confidence as well as style. It's like buying furniture—what looks great on the showroom floor may be the wrong color or fit for your living room. So when you buy something pricey (be sure to check the store's return policy), bring it home, and try it on again (leave the tags on). Do you like the way it makes you feel? Does it move comfortably with your body? Will it suit all your needs? What does your style buddy think? Doing this will help you avoid costly mistakes. Now, don't abuse this exercise; use it only when necessary.

PUT YOUR LOOK BOOK TOGETHER

Now that you have edited your closet, found what works for you, and purchased what was missing, it's time to put together your look book (page 119). Spend a weekend putting on the different outfits or looks that you have discovered work great for you and taking digital photographs of each one, then download them to your computer for future reference. On those days when you are feeling sluggish and uninspired, flip through your look book and then put on an outfit that you love. Soon you won't even need to glance at the book; your style will have become second nature.

BECOME A STYLIST

Don't you find it's often easy to tell other people what looks good on them but you're clueless when it comes to yourself? That's because you know your flaws (or perceived flaws) intimately but don't see theirs. So practice style on your friend, mom, or sister. It's much easier to mix patterns and colors on someone else, when you're not the one taking the risk. What does watching her try on clothes make you realize about your own style? Then, when it's your turn, ask her to be your style consultant.

hold that pose

To look good every time you have your picture taken, you have to figure out how to stand, which side of your face to show the camera, whether your head should be up or down, etc. Have a friend take lots of pictures of you with a digital camera so you can decide. There's a reason celebrities always strike the same poses on the red carpet—they know that's how they look the best. You should do the same. Look at pictures of yourself that you like and notice where the light source is coming from. Try to recreate that lighting all the time (and not just when posing for pictures.)

Style in an instant

What are your instant style secrets? Fishnet tights? Animal-print flats? A designer scarf? Figure out five to ten items that give you instant style and keep them on hand.

HOST A STYLE PARTY

We all have clothes and accessories that don't fit or look right, but somehow we just can't bear to part with them. As if your feet will actually shrink and you'll be able to wear those too-small-but-too-fabulous heels you adore! And in the back of your closet there's that flowered handkerchief skirt that looks ridiculous on you, but you keep it because you bought it on a Caribbean vacation with an ex-boyfriend you still remember fondly.

Sometimes it's just time to let go of things. Have a party. Invite a bunch of girlfriends over for a drink, and tell them they each have to bring ten items—clothes and accessories—that they love but no longer wear. Try on each other's stuff, and if something looks great—everyone will have an opinion—they can take it home. What doesn't go to someone else's closet goes to the thrift store.

it's the little things

There are plenty of modestly priced treats you can give yourself to feel stylish. Have your hair washed and blown dry by the hairdresser or have your makeup done before an evening out. Watch what stylists do so you learn something. Get your eyebrows professionally threaded or tweezed. Have an exfoliating body scrub at a day spa. Buy a fabulous bra-and-undies set—you'll feel good, even if no one else sees it.

I CAN DO THAT

Play a fashion game every so often: Find an outfit or a look in a fashion magazine that you love and then try to re-create it from your own closet. You might be surprised to discover what's lurking in your wardrobe.

INSIDE AS WELL AS OUT

Yeah, exercise is part of taking care of yourself. Jacob Jansen, a personal trainer at Crunch Fitness, suggests that women change up their routines every two to four weeks. Your body becomes acclimated to the same routine, and results decrease if you do the same thing over and over. Be sure to mix your cardiovascular workout with lifting weights. Just like fashion, you have to mix up your fitness style. Here are some of Jacob's suggestions:

• Use free weights. Dumbbells and barbells can help sculpt your muscles quickly.

• When lifting free weights, do compound movements: Use weights while performing squats, lunges, leg lifts, dead lifts, etc. Compound movements require more muscle activity than single-joint movements.

• Lift heavier weights and do fewer reps. Put down those two-pound pink dumbbells! Use a heavier weight that you can lift six to eight times in a row. By the eighth rep, you should really be working hard to lift the weight. By keeping the rep count low and the weight high, you can build muscle (not bulk)

and increase your metabolism.

• Mix it up! Get off the elliptical trainer and jump rope or take a spinning class. Try boxing instead of step class. Walk or jog on the treadmill for a minute, then sprint for another one. Repeat. Build up each time, so you are sprinting more than walking.

• Hire a personal trainer. Throughout this book, I have talked about when it is important to spend money. This is one of those times. If you can't afford regular sessions with a trainer, work for several sessions with someone who can develop a program just for you.

Still on the hunt for that perfect pair of jeans? Devote a day to going from store to store and trying on every pair of jeans. Just jeans. Nothing else. You can look at dresses another day. Hunt for evening shoes at yet another time.

And trying them on doesn't mean just slipping into a pair, looking over your shoulder at your tush, and saying they're fine. Trying them on means standing, walking, and sitting in them, as well as looking at them from every possible angle. A pattern of what looks best on you will emerge. Most important, which jeans make you feel good? Which ones make you shudder in horror? The ones that make you smile and feel just right are the ones to buy.

Use this shopping trick for everything: dresses, tops, sweaters, pants, and bras. If you stay focused on shopping for just one thing, you will be successful.

Make an Event out of Getting Ready

We all know that getting ready can be a challenge, especially for a big event. Learn to give yourself the gift of time and leisure when dressing for an occasion. If you have kids, tell the babysitter to come an hour earlier or let your husband watch them until you're ready. Close your bedroom door, pour yourself a glass of wine, put on your favorite music, and dance around the room. Set the mood and tone by putting on your makeup, doing your hair, and stepping into your clothes in a serene environment. If you have fun while getting ready, you'll look better and feel more confident when you walk out the door. It's as much an effort to have fun as it is to have style. The two are synonymous, and the more you learn that lesson the more style and fun you'll have.

E C O · S T Y L E

We only have one earth. Challenge yourself to discover eco-friendly ways to have style. Buy clothes made of hemp, bamboo, or organic cotton. There are even eco-friendly fabrics made from recycled plastic bottles!

If you and your friends all get the same five fashion magazines, get rid of all but one subscription and share them among yourselves.

Cancel all those catalogs that are stuffed into your mailbox. (Check out sites such as catalogchoice.org or directmail.com that let you opt out of unwanted mail.)

Keep an Eco-Bag in your handbag to fill with your purchases when shopping. Say, "No, thank you," to the salesperson when a shopping bag is offered. You have enough of those.

acknowledgments

● ● ● ● ● ● ●

I don't know what or who convinced me that I had enough style to teach others about the subject, but somehow I've always been opinionated and honest to the point where people listened. It started in my youth, when I told my mom, my sisters, my aunts, and female acquaintances what to wear and with which shoes. I have no idea what made me so confident in my taste, but there I was—a chubby little boy dictating style to the women in my neighborhood. I thank those who sought my counsel then and set the tone for the rest of my life. And a special thanks to my mom, the queen of style.

This book wouldn't have been possible without a lot of other people, and I'd like to thank them: Bill Shinker and Lauren Marino at Gotham Books, who believed in my ideas. Korey Provencher and Harriet Bell for steering the ship. Jason Frank Rothenberg for having the beautiful eye and capturing the process on film. Peter Buchanan-Smith for guiding us on a sea of beautifully designed pages. Ashley Javier, Ryan Cotton, and Mally Roncal for collaborating on hair and makeup. Kristen Naiman, who styled tirelessly, doing and undoing and doing again. The twelve wonderful women who let me run their lives for however long it took to grow out their bangs; they were all good sports.

My biggest thank-you goes to Marisa Gardini, who facilitated this book, along with everything I do. Marisa inspires me and shows me how to have style.

Thank you to everyone behind the scenes who made this book possible:

Alla Katkov
Amanda Sinclair
Anna Wintour
Bernardo Aguirre
Brianne Ramagosa
Christine Fulwiler
Claudia De Sousa
Deborah Weiss-Geline
Donna Karan
Elizabeth Kennedy
Erika Stair
Everyone at 475
Fanny Mavridis
Gail Oliver
George Perkins
Iman
Jacob Jansen
Janicza Bravo
Jayne Harkness
Jeff Chastain
Jeff Stark
Jennifer Lurie
Jessica Wendrychowicz
Jill Bream
Jon Shireman
Josef Reyes
Kristina Critchlow
Judith Sutton
Lili Dialou
Linda Nova
Marilu Menendez, Lord & Taylor
Meghan Horstmann
Nancy Bittan, Henry Hanger Company
Niki Turkington, The Brooks Group
Patrick O'Connell
Patti Cohen
Sally Cunningham
Sam Wilson
Sarah Moran
Shannon O'Hara
Shawn Hasto
Stephanie Noritz
Tatiana Cobian
Zoe Rosenfeld

acknowledgments

• • • • • • •

A huge thank-you to all the companies, designers, and stores that donated, lent, and contributed clothing and accessories to the making of *How to Have Style:*

Adidas

Aigle

Anthropologie

A Second Chance

Bag Borrow or Steal:
www.BagBorroworSteal.com

Bali

Banana Republic Worldwide:
www.BananaRepublic.com
for locations

Barefoot Tess: www.barefootess.com

BillyKirk Bags

Bradbury Lewis (Steven Alan and
Hayden Harnett)

Bromley Group

Calvin Klein

Calypso

Cartier
Available at Cartier boutiques
nationwide. For further
information, please call 1-800-
CARTIER or visit www.cartier.com

Castor & Pollux

Champion Nationwide Order Lines:
1-800-315-0563/24 hours a day,
7 days a week

Club Monaco

Coldwater Creek

Company Agenda (Kork-Ease)

Cosabella, Corporate Headquarters,
12186 SW 128th Street,
Miami, FL 33186 (305-253-9904)

Danielle Stevens

Dashing Diva

DKNY

Donna Karan Collection

Doyle & Doyle dog and heart
charm bracelet (99992340B), $575

Earnest Sewn

Eberjey

Finn Jewelry: www.finnjewelry.com,
available at Barney's New York

Firm fannies and trim tummies
courtesy of SPANX shapewear
and hosiery

Fogal of Switzerland,
515 Madison Avenue,
New York, NY

Frederick's of Hollywood

Gap Worldwide: www.gap.com and
at stores nationwide

Giordano

Giuseppe Zanotti Design

Hanro

Henry Hanger Company

House of Lavande,
Palm Beach;
www.houseoflavande.com

IGIGI, available in sizes 12–32 at
www.igigi.com

Isaac Mizrahi New York

Joan Hornig Jewelry

Kate Spade

Kenneth Jay Lane

Kiki de Montparnasse

KMR (Tummy Tuck Jeans)

Krupp Group (Melissa Joy Manning
and Philip Crangi)

La Force + Stevens (Milly)

La Perla

Levi's Jeans

London Sole

Lord & Taylor

Loro Piana Bellevue Bag: for store
locations see www.loropiana.com

Maidenform

Matta,
241 Lafayette Street,
New York, NY 10012,
212-343-9399

Miano Viél Salon and Spa

Michael Teperson:
www.michaelteperson.com

MSPR

NY&CO

Old Navy

Only Hearts

Paul Wilmot for Karen Rodriguez

RAW Information Group

Shoes provided by Converse

Steve Madden

Target®

Ted Muehling, New York, NY

Tiffany & Co.: 800-526-0649

Time Will Tell Watches

Torrid
(Delia Douglas and
Martha Muehlmann)

Tucker

Urban Outfitters

Verdura

UNIQLO: 877-4-UNIQLO or
customer.orders@uniqlo-usa.com

Verdura

Wacoal

Wolford

Wonderbra

Zero

my favorite places

• • • • • • •

Here are some of the shops, boutiques, and other stores that I adore or inspire me.
Check them out and see what they do for you.

• • • • • • •

BEST BASICS

Agnès B
New York, Los Angeles, San
Francisco
www.agnesb.net

A.P.C.
131 Mercer St.
New York, NY 10012
(212) 966-0069
www.apc.fr

Club Monaco
www.clubmonaco.com

Gap
www.gap.com

J. Crew
www.jcrew.com

Levi's
www.levisstore.com

Macy's
www.macys.com

Old Navy
www.oldnavy.com

Theory
www.theory.com

uniqlo
546 Broadway
New York, NY 10012
(917) 237-8880
www.uniqlo.com

• • • • • • •

BOHEMIAN LUXE

Calypso
815 Madison Ave.
New York, NY 10065
(212) 585-0310
www.calypso-celle.com

• • • • • • •

BOUTIQUES

Albertine
13 Christopher St.
New York, NY 10014
(212) 924-8515

Bird
220 Smith St.
Brooklyn, NY 11201
(718) 797-3774
www.shopbird.com

Bows and Arrows
215 S. Lamar, Suite C
Austin, TX 78704
www.shopbowsplusarrows.com

Castor and Pollux
238 W. 10th St.
New York, NY 10014
(212) 645-6572
www.castorandpolluxstore.com

Creatures of Comfort
7971 Melrose Ave.
Los Angeles, CA 90046
(323) 655-7855
www.creaturesofcomfort.us

Fred Segal
420 & 500 Broadway
Santa Monica, CA 90401
(310) 394-9814
www.fredsegal.com

Jake
3740 N. Southport Ave.
Chicago, IL 60613
(773) 929-5253
www.shopjake.com

Louis Boston
234 Berkeley St.
Boston, MA 02116
(617) 262-6100
www.louisboston.com

Kick Pleat
918 W. 12th St.
Austin, TX 78703
(512) 445-4500
www.kickpleat.com

Matta
241 Lafayette St.
New York, NY 10012
(212) 343-9399
www.mattany.com

Olive & Bette's
1070 Madison Ave.
New York, NY 10028
(212) 717-9655
www.oliveandbettes.com

Palm on Park
444 4th St.
Boca Grande, FL 33921
(941) 964-4448
www.thepalmonpark.com

Satine
8117 W. 3rd St.
Los Angeles, CA 90048
(323) 655-2142
www.satineboutique.com

Scoop
www.scoopnyc.com

Skirt
931 W. Lancaster Ave.
Bryn Mawr, PA 19010
(610) 520-0222

Steven Alan
New York, Los Angeles
www.stevenalan.com

• • • • • • •

CHEAP THRILLS

Century 21
New York, New Jersey
www.c21stores.com

H&M
www.hm.com

Loehmann's
www.loehmanns.com

Target®
www.target.com

Top Shop
478 Broadway
New York, NY 10013
(212) 302-4351
www.topshop.com

my favorite places

· · · · · · ·

Pearl River Mart
477 Broadway
New York, NY 10013
(212) 431-4770
www.pearlriver.com

Zara
www.zara.com

· · · · · · ·

CHIC BOUTIQUES

Capitol
6815 Phillips Place Ct.
Charlotte, NC 28210
(704) 552-8987

Dighton Rhode
5 Lewis St.
Greenwich, CT 06830
(203) 622-4600
www.dightonrhode.com

Hirshleifer's
2080 Northern Blvd.
Manhasset, NY 11030
(516) 627-3566
www.hirshleifers.com

Hitchcock
1123 34th Ave.
Seattle, WA 98122
(206) 838-7173
www.shophitchcock.com

Jamie
4317 Harding Rd.
Nashville, TN 37205
(615) 292-4188
www.jamie-nashville.com

Ikram
873 N. Rush St.
Chicago, IL 60611
(312) 587-1000
www.ikram.com

L'Armoire
102 Park St.
New Canaan, CT 06840
(203) 966-1764
www.larmoirenewcanaan.com

Mary Jane Denzer
222 Mamaroneck Ave.
White Plains, NY 10605
(914) 328-0330
www.maryjanedenzer.com

Saks Jandel
2522 Virginia Ave. NW
Washington, DC 20037
(310) 652-2250

Sharon Batten
330 Highway A1A N, Suite 212
Ponte Vedra Beach, FL 32082
(904) 285-4544
www.sharonbatten.com

Stanley Korshak
500 Crescent Ct. #100
Dallas, TX 75201
(214) 871-3600
www.stanleykorshak.com

Wilkes Bashford
375 Sutter St.
San Francisco, CA 94108
(415) 986-4380
www.wilkesbashford.com

· · · · · · ·

COSTUME JEWELRY

Kenneth Jay Lane
www.kennethjaylane.net

Alexis Bittar
465 Broome St
New York, NY 10013
(212) 625-8340
www.alexisbittar.com

Time Will Tell
P.O. Box 51998
New Orleans, LA 70151
(504) 376-3636
www.timewilltellwatches.com

· · · · · · ·

DEPARTMENT STORES

Bergdorf Goodman
754 5th Ave.
New York, NY 10019
(212) 753-7300
www.bergdorfgoodman.com

Bloomingdales
www.bloomingdales.com

Lord & Taylor
www.lordandtaylor.com

Neiman Marcus
www.neimanmarcus.com

Nordstrom
www.nordstrom.com

Saks Fifth Avenue
www.saksfifthavenue.com

· · · · · · ·

FINE JEWELRY

Ted Muehling
27 Howard St.
New York, NY 10013
(212) 431-3825
www.tedmuehling.com

Doyle & Doyle
189 Orchard St.
New York, NY 10002
(212) 677-9991
www.doyledoyle.com

Melissa Joy Manning
www.melissajoymanning.com

· · · · · · ·

FOUL-WEATHER GEAR

Aigle
www.aigleboots.com

Burberry
www.burberry.com

Barbour
www.barbour.com

L.L. Bean
www.llbean.com

my favorite places

• • • • • • •

INSTANT STYLE

Anthropologie
www.anthropologie.com

Paul Smith
142 Greene St.
New York, NY 10012
(212) 254-3530
www.paulsmith.co.uk

Urban Outfitters
www.urbanoutfitters.com

UNDERGARMENTS

Bra Tenders
630 9th Ave. #601
New York, NY 10036
(212) 957-7000
www.bratenders.com

Cosabella
www.cosabella.com

Falke
www.falke.co.za

Fogal
515 Madison Ave.
New York, NY 10022
(212) 355-3254
www.fogal.com

Hue
www.hue.com

Kiki De Montparnasse
79 Greene St.
New York, NY 10012
(212) 965-8070
www.kikidm.com

Only Hearts
www.onlyhearts.com

Petite Coquette
51 University Pl.
New York, NY 10003
(212) 473-2478
www.thelittleflirt.com

Wacoal
www.wacoal-america.com

LEATHER GOODS

Coach
www.coach.com

Hermès
www.hermes.com

Kate Spade
www.katespade.com

Roger Vivier
www.rogervivier.com

ONLINE RESOURCES

Bag Borrow or Steal
www.BagBorroworSteal.com

eBay
www.ebay.com

Net-a-Porter
www.net-a-porter.com

Shop Intuition
www.shopintuition.com

Refinery 29
www.refinery29.com

PERFUME

Aedes de Venusta
9 Christopher St.
New York, NY 10014
(212) 206-8674
www.aedes.com

Jo Malone
www.jomalone.com

Chanel
www.chanel.com

Santa Maria Novella
285 Lafayette St.
New York, NY 10012
(212) 925-0001
www.lafcony.com

SHOES

Barefoot Tess
(large sizes)
www.barefoottess.com

Christian Louboutin
www.christianlouboutin.fr

Converse
www.converse.com

Giordanos
(sizes 4 – 5 1/2 only)
1150 2nd Ave.
New York, NY 10065
(212) 688-7195
www.petiteshoes.com

Keds
www.keds.com

Nine West
www.ninewest.com

Sigerson Morrison
www.sigersonmorrison.com

PLACES FOR INSPIRATION

Barneys New York
660 Madison Avenue
New York, NY 10065
(212) 754-7940
www. barneys.com

Comme des Garcons
520 W. 22nd St.
New York, NY 10011
(212) 604-9200

Estella
493 6th Ave.
New York, NY 10011
(212) 255-3553
www.estella-nyc.com

my favorite places

· · · · · · ·

Jeffrey
449 W. 14th St.
New York, NY 10014
(212) 206-3928
www.jeffreynewyork.com

Marimekko
1262 3rd Ave.
New York NY 10021
(212) 628-8400
www.marimekko.com

Museum of Modern Art Store
44 W. 53rd St.
New York, NY 10019
(212) 767-1050
www.momastore.com

Moss
150 Greene St.
New York, NY 10012
(212) 204-7100
www.mossonline.com

Niketown
6 E. 57th St.
New York, NY 10022
(212) 891-6453
www.nike.com

Prada
www.prada.com

The Conran Shop
407 E. 59th St.
New York, NY 10022
(212) 755-9079
www.conranusa.com
Williams-Sonoma
www.williams-sonoma.com

· · · · · · ·

PLUS SIZES

Coldwater Creek
www.coldwatercreek.com

Marina Rinaldi
800 Madison Ave.
New York, NY 10065
(212) 734-4333

NY&C
www.nyandcompany.com

Torrid
www.torrid.com

Tummy Tuck Jeans
www.tummytuckjeans.com

· · · · · · ·

SCARVES

Chanel
www.chanel.com

R by 45rpm
169 Mercer St.
New York, NY 10012
(917) 237-0045
www.rby45rpm.com

Turnbull and Asser
New York, Los Angeles
www.turnbullandasser.com

· · · · · · ·

NEW YORK DESIGNERS

Tucker by Gabby Basora
www.tuckerbygabybasora.com

Zero Maria Cornejo
807 Greenwich St.
New York, NY 10014
(212) 620-0460
www.zeromariacornejo.com

Built by Wendy
7 Centre Market Pl.
New York, NY 10013
(212) 925-6538
www.builtbywendy.com

· · · · · · ·

VINTAGE

A Second Chance
1109 Lexington Ave. #2
New York, NY 10075
(212) 744-6041
www.asecondchanceresale.com

C. Madeleine's
13702 Biscayne Blvd.
N. Miami, FL 33181
(305) 945-7770
shop.cmadeleines.com

Fisch for the Hip
153 W. 18th St.
New York, NY 10011
(212) 633-9053
www.fischforthehip.com

Fluke
86 N. 6th Street
Brooklyn, NY 11211
(718) 486-3166

Housing Works
www.housingworks.org

Sweet Tater
280 Mulberry St.
New York, NY 10012
(212) 219-6400
www.sweettater.net

The Way We Wore
334 S. La Brea Ave.
Los Angeles, CA 90036
(323) 937-0878
www.thewaywewore.com

· · · · · · ·

WORTH THE SPLURGE

Bottega Veneta
www.bottegaveneta.com

Cartier
www.cartier.com

Louis Vuitton
www.vuitton.com

credits

• • • • • • •

MANNING FAIREY

Page 38, clockwise from top left:
Loeffler Randall for Target ® red patent
slingbacks/Isaac Mizrahi for Target®
platform pumps/Hollwould for Target®
red open-toe heels/ Hollwould for Target®
black heels/Isaac Mizrahi for Target®
mules/Isaac Mizrahi for Target® flats

Page 40, left: Levi's jeans/Isaac Mizrahi
for Target® hoodie and coat/Dolce
& Gabbana bra from Century 21/
Barefoottess.com Keds/Urban
Outfitters scarf

Page 40, right: Marni skirt eBay.com/Brooks
Brothers boy's blazer/J. Crew skirt/Lord
& Taylor pocket square/Isaac Mizrahi for
Target® shoes/Anthropologie bracelets

Page 41, left: Brooks Brothers boy's tuxedo/
Isaac Mizrahi for Target® shoes

Page 41, right: Anthropologie skirt/Isaac
Mizrahi for Target® sweater/Hollwould
for Target ® shoes

JANINE GARDNER

Page 49: Paul Smith raincoat/Fendi handbag
from bagborroworsteal.com

Page 52, left: Philip Lim skirt/Paul Smith
sweater/Giordano's shoes/Chanel scarf/
Nancy Gonzalez handbag/Ted Muehling
earrings

Page 52, right: uniqlo jeans, jacket and shirt/
Mark Jacobs watch/ Louis Vuitton Papillon
handbag

Page 53, left: Alberta Ferretti dress/Paul Smith
sweater/Celine shoes/Gap belt/Fendi
handbag

Page 53, right: Alberta Ferretti skirt/
Pollini jacket/Giordano's shoes/Ralph
Lauren belt

BIANCA GOMEZ

Page 58: kate spade suitcase

Page 62: Calypso turquoise dress

Page 64, left: Levi's jeans/DKNY coat and
blazer/Isaac Mizrahi for Target® sweater/
Virginia Johnson wrap/Minnetonka
moccasins/Sweet Tater vintage handbag/
Selima Optique sunglasses

Page 64, right: DKNY suit/uniqlo shirt/
Repetto shoes/Cartier tank watch

Page 65: Zero Maria Cornejo dress/Urban
Outfitters earrings

LISA TAYLOR

Page 76, left: Matta caftan/Bernardo sandals/
Verdura necklace and cuffs

Page 76, right: Levi's jeans/Marimekko t-shirt/
Ralph Lauren jacket/Barefoottess.com
shoes/Hermés scarf

Page 77, left: Ellen Tracy jacket/Hanes tank
top/Bernardo sandals

Page 77, right: Isaac Mizrahi New York dress
and shoes/Michael Teperson clutch/House
of Lavande vintage earrings

BROOKE FERN

Page 83: A.P.C. jeans/Anthropologie sweater/
Converse sneakers/Barefoottess.com red
shoes/J. Crew bracelets

Page 84: Anthropologie skirt/Frye shoes/Isaac
Mizrahi for Target® pink-purple-gold tote/
Lord & Taylor handbag/J. Crew belt

Page 87, left: Mason gold jacket/earnest
sewn denim skirt

Page 87, right: Anthropologie denim dress/
Banana Republic faux fur denim jacket/
vintage brooch

Page 88: Ralph Lauren skirt/H & M blouse/
Delman shoes/Betsey Johnson belt/
J. Crew bangle bracelets

Page 89, left: A.P.C. jeans/Lacoste shirt/
ernestsewn jacket/Calypso scarf/
Marimekko handbag/Bernardo sandals

Page 89, right: Gap skirt/vintage jacket/uniqlo
turtleneck/Sweet Tater vintage boots/
Hermés handbag/ DKNY tights

MARY KATE GAUDET

Page 94: Coldwater Creek blouse and
sweater/Tummy Tuck Jeans/agnès
b. shoes/Tracy Reese handbag from
bagborrowsteal.com/Marc Jacobs watch

Page 96: Igigi dress/Sigerson Morrison shoes/
Mayle handbag

Page 98, left: Torrid skirt/Igigi jacket/
Hollwould for Target® shoes/Michel
Perry clutch

Page 98, right: uniqlo sweater/Ellen Tracy
jacket/Christian Louboutin shoes/Lord &
Taylor handbag/Chanel scarf

Page 99: Tripp tank top/Wacoal bra

LARA HALL

Page 105: Club Monaco suit/J. Crew blouse/
Miu Miu handbag and shoes/Oscar de la
Renta scarf

Page 108: Calypso jeans/J. Crew tank top
and sweater

Page 109, left: Ralph Lauren black-and-red
top/Bernardo sandals

Page 109, right: J. Crew polka shoe/
Wacoal bra

Page 110: DKNY jacket/Calypso scarf

Page 111, left: Chaiken dress/J. Crew clutch/
Christian Louboutin shoes/Philip Crangi
earrings

Page 111, right: Mina Stone dress/J. Crew
clutch/ Verdura bracelets/J. Crew ring

SUSAN CLAXTON

Page 125, left to right: Paul Smith dress/
vintage dress/Calypso dress/L'Autre Chose
flats/Giuseppe Zanotti heels

Page 126: Fendi handbag from
bagborroworsteal.com/Christian
Louboutin mules

credits

• • • • • • •

Page 128, left: Urban Outfitters dress/Philip
    Lim coat/Tracey Reese boots/Chanel
    Handbag from bagborrowandsteal.com/
    Hue tights
Page 128, right: Susan's own skirt, coat, and
    scarf/J. Crew sweater/Kara Voss clutch
Page 129, left: Susan's own pants and jacket/
    J. Crew sweater/Wolford turtleneck
Page 129, right: Lanvin vintage dress, private
    collection/Alexis Bittar red necklace/agnès
    b. turquoise necklace

KERI KEANE

Page 134: Chlöe sweater/Only Hearts
    camisole
Page 137: Coach coat/J. Crew skirt/Hermés
    vintage handbag from bagborroworsteal.
    com/Kork-Ease shoes/Hanes tank top
Page 139: Isaac Mizrahi for Target® dress/
    Christian Louboutin shoes/Danielle
    Stevens jewelry
Page 141, left: Banana Republic skirt/uniqlo
    sweater/Frye boots/hat, private collection
Page 141, right: Banana Republic dress/Isaac
    Mizrahi for Target® boots/Hollwould for
    Target® handbag

SUSAN SHAPIRO

Page 151: Jewelry, private collections
Page 155: Isaac Mizrahi New York gown

REGAN MURPHY

Page 164: Theory suit/Michel Perry boots/
    Louis Vuitton handbag
Page 167, top right: Anthropologie dress/
    Milly coat/Fry Shoes
Page 170: agnès b. trousers and blouse/
    uniqlo sweater/Gucci belt
Page 171, left: uniqlo shorts, jacket, and
    sweater/Isaac Mizrahi for Target® coat/
    agnès b. shoes/Fogal tights
Page 171, right: Calvin Klein dress/Frye shoes

REBECCA FRAZER

Page 176: Milly jacket
Page 178: Anna Sui skirt/Only Hearts
    camisole/uniqlo jacket/agnès b. handbag/
    Isaac Mizrahi for Target® boots
Page 180, left: Milly skirt/Urban Outfitters
    sweater/Hollwould for Target® shoes/
    Wacoal bra
Page 180, right: ABS dress/Ann Taylor
    handbag/What Goes Around Comes
    Around gloves/Hollwould for Target®
    shoes/Fogal tights
Page 181: Isaac Mizrahi New York dress/
    Sigerson Morrison shoes/Lord and Taylor
    clutch

WHAT YOU NEED

SHOES

Page 184: Aigle rain boots/cowboy boots,
    private collection/Isaac Mizrahi New York
    black boots
Page 185: Casadei ankle strap sandals/Frye
    t-strap heels/ Isaac Mizrahi New York black
    pumps/ Isaac Mizrahi New York jeweled
    evening sandals/Nine West animal print
    heels/Giuseppe Zanotti evening heels
Page 186: Belgian Shoes Lui/London Sole
    ballet flats/Christian Louboutin wedge
    sandals/Urban Outfitters Mary Janes
Page 187: Tod's driving shoes/Havaiana flip
    flops/Converse sneakers/ J. Crew metallic
    flip flops

BAGS

Page 188: J. Crew madras bag/Roger Vivier
    evening clutch/Loro Piano everyday tote
    bag/Coach everyday shoulder bag
Page 189: A.P.C. pocketbook/kate spade
    computer tote/Louis Vuitton/Eco-Bag,
    private collection/Filson weekend tote

JEWELRY

Page 190: Joan Hornig pearls on a wire/
    Fragments chandelier earrings/Melissa
    Joy Manning gold hoops/Banana Republic
    costume band ring
Page 191: Doyle & Doyle vintage charm
    bracelet/Cartier splurge bangle bracelets/
    Urban Outfitters and H&M inexpensive
    bangle bracelets/Tom Binns statement cuff
Page 193: House of Lavande pearls/Kenneth
    Jay Lane statement necklace/Philip Crangi
    acorn necklace, heart necklace, private
    collection, Banana Republic disk necklace

WATCHES

Pages 194 and 195, left to right: Cartier
    tank watch/Time Will Tell red watch/
    ToyWatch large diver's watch/man's watch
    and diamond evening watch, private
    collection/Verdura pineapple watch/
    Rolex watch

BRAS

Page 197: Kiki de Montparnasse bra/
    Champion sports bra
Page 198, top to bottom: Only Hearts
    strapless/Only Hearts outerwear bra/Only
    Hearts black lace bra/Wacoal contour bra
Page 199: Spanx Bra-llelujah/La Perla peek-
    a-boo bra/ Wacoal underwire seamed
    bra/racerback bra (unavailable)

INSTANT STYLE IDEAS

Page 200: sunglasses, private collection/
    Theory white shirt/cocktail ring, private
    collection/J.Crew sweaters
Page 201: A.P.C. trench coat/House of
    Lavande chandelier earrings/Fogal tights/
    Christian Louboutin black pump

LOSE PAUNCH!

Hair: SLIMMER + TALLER

AIRBRUSH AIRBRUSH AIRBRUSH.

BODY: SLIMMER + TALLER

Heels?

Isaac Mizrahi is a Libra. He plays bridge and is devoted to his beloved collie-mix dog named Harry. He has been designing clothes for twenty years and has been awarded four CFDA awards, including a special award in 1996 for the groundbreaking documentary *Unzipped*. In 2002 Isaac began a successful collaboration with Target® designing apparel and home furnishings. Isaac is presently the Creative Director for the Liz Claiborne brand. In 2000, he wrote and starred in *Les Mizrahi*, an off-Broadway show. Isaac has created costumes for movies, theatre, dance, and opera. Television audiences have come to love Isaac as the host of his own series on the Oxygen Network and the Style Network.